Implementing the Electronic Health Record:
Case Studies and Strategies for Success

Edited by Joe Miller, MA, FHIMSS

HIMSS Mission

To lead change in the healthcare information and management systems field through knowledge sharing, advocacy, collaboration, innovation, and community affiliations.

Printed in the U.S.A. 5 4 3 2 1

Requests for permission to reproduce any part of this work should be sent to:
Permissions Editor
HIMSS
230 E. Ohio St., Suite 500
Chicago, IL 60611-3269
nvitucci@himss.org

The inclusion of an organization name, product or service in this publication should not be considered as an endorsement of such organization, product or service, nor is the failure to include an organization name, product or service to be construed as disapproval.

ISBN 0-9761277-1-7

For more information about HIMSS, please visit www.himss.org.

About the Editor

Joe Miller, MA, FHIMSS, is Manager of Information Services at Christiana Care Health System in Wilmington, Delaware, where he is responsible for the implementation of key components of the organization's EHR including clinical documentation, order management, and clinical decision support. Since 2000 he has chaired the HIMSS Computer-based Patient Record SIG (special interest group). He is a member of the HIMSS EHR Steering Committee and Chair of the EHR Toolkit Taskforce. In 2002–2003 Mr. Miller presented a series of highly regarded workshops, panel discussions and audio conferences on implementing computerized provider order entry. He has also served as faculty at the Annual HIMSS Conference & Exhibition on the HL7 standard and the relationship of the EHR to the legal health record.

For the most up-to-date information on HIMSS' visioning, advocacy and support for the EHR, go to www.himss.org and search for 'EHR.'

Contributors

Margaret (Peggy) Budnik, DM, RN, is Project Lead for Clinical Application at Saint Francis Health System, Tulsa, Oklahoma. She has over 35 years of nursing experience, holding a variety of positions over the years including bedside nursing, nursing management and administration, and nursing education. Dr. Budnik also has over 15 years of experience as a pioneer in the field of nursing informatics. Her current position includes managing the implementation and support of a clinical information system where she primarily focuses on nursing and physician utilization of a clinical system in the acute care setting. Dr. Budnik is recognized as an expert on healthcare informatics, speaking regularly at regional and national healthcare informatics programs.

Toby Clark, RPh, MSc, FASHP, is a medication systems consultant and Clinical Associate Professor of Pharmacy Practice at Medical University of South Carolina in Charleston. Previously he has served as (Adjunct) Professor of Pharmacy Practice and Director of Pharmacy (retired) at the University of Illinois at Chicago College of Pharmacy and Medical Center. Clark's professional interests are focused on the safety, quality, and productivity of the medication system. A nationally recognized expert and frequent lecturer on topics of pharmacy/medication system informatics and computerized provider order entry, he spearheaded formation of the group POE-CPOE list serve, now operated by the American Society of Health-System Pharmacists. Clark is a past chair of the University HealthSystem Consortium Pharmacy Council and has served in a leadership role in state and national hospital pharmacy organizations. He strongly advocates hospital pharmacists serving patients through the safety and quality of medication system.

Edward Ewen, MD, FACP, is Director of Clinical Informatics for Christiana Care Health System. He attended medical school at the University of Illinois in Chicago and completed his post graduate training in Internal Medicine at Northwestern University. He joined Christiana Care in 1988 as Director of Ambulatory Services and Medical Consult Services and remains actively involved in graduate medical education and clinical practice. In 1997 Dr. Ewen led Christiana Care's efforts to design and implement a custom data warehouse, aggregating information from across the system's health plans and provider operations. In 1998 he became Director of Disease Management and Chief Medical Officer of the Christiana Care Physician Organization, and in 1999 he assumed the role of Director of Clinical Informatics. Dr. Ewen is also an active participant in the design and development of the Delaware Health Information Network, Delaware's regional health information initiative.

Matt Handley, MD, is Associate Medical Director, Quality and Informatics, Group Health Cooperative—one of the nation's largest consumer-governed healthcare systems. Dr. Handley is responsible for quality improvement and technology, working to create an infrastructure that supports the highest levels of organizational performance. He has been a physician with Group Health since 1984, and maintains a primary care practice at the Family Health Medical Center at the Capitol Hill Campus in Seattle. Previously, Dr. Handley was Medical Director of Health Informatics at Group Health, overseeing the implementation and management of the clinical information system. He also directed the development the now 5,000-page, Group Health clinical Web site. Dr. Handley has worked with groups around the country to develop clinical guideline programs and lectured extensively on topics including evidence-based medicine, implementation of clinical guidelines, cardiovascular disease prevention, prostate cancer screening, and hepatitis C. Dr. Handley attended Northwestern University where he studied biomedical engineering and applied mathematics. He received his MD at the University of California at Davis and completed residency training in family practice at Group Health.

Fanny Hawkins, EdD, RHIA, CPHQ, is Director of the Health Information Management Program at Texas Southern University. Her work focuses on evaluating clinical data in the EMR and EMR Project Management. Dr. Hawkins is recently completing a Fellowship in Health Informatics at Baylor College of Medicine with a primary focus on implementing the EMR in an ambulatory setting.

Laura Jantos, MBA, MHA, FHIMSS, is the principal of ECG Management Consultants, Inc.'s national Healthcare IT practice. She has more than 15 years of experience assisting healthcare organizations in planning for, selecting, and implementing appropriate technologies, with particular expertise in electronic health records (EHRs). Ms. Jantos' practice focuses on system strategy and implementation. She is regularly engaged by leaders of complex healthcare environments to facilitate the development and implementation of a clear, actionable plan for IT. She has assisted clients in coaching CIOs, providing interim leadership to IS departments and critical projects, creating physician/hospital integration strategy, and establishing an organization-wide project management competency. In addition to her work with EHRs, Ms. Jantos also has expertise in financial and business systems, Picture Archiving and Communication Systems (PACS), and hospital information systems.

Donald Levick, MD, MBA, is a practicing pediatrician and the Physician Liaison for the Information Services Department of Lehigh Valley Hospital. As physician liaison, he acts as the primary contact between the medical staff and the IS department. He is also involved in the planning and implementation of the several IT projects, including CPOE, an ambulatory EMR, a critical care information system, data repositories and evidence-based medicine. Dr. Levick is the President of the Medical Staff of Lehigh Valley Hospital, and previously served as the Chairman of the Board of Governors and Associate Medical Director of the Lehigh Valley Physician Group (the employed physician group of Lehigh Valley Hospital). He has experience in strategic planning and leading change at multiple organizational levels. He has spoken nationally on CPOE and change management.

Eric M. Liederman, MD, MPH, is Medical Director for Clinical Information Systems at the UC Davis Health System, where he has implemented an electronic health record (EHR), which includes secure web-based patient-physician communications, digital radiology image distribution system, electronic order entry and documentation, and a clinical data repository. Dr. Liederman currently serves as clinician leader of the interactive design, knowledge management/clinical decision support, patient empowerment and privacy protection efforts for UC Davis' EHR project. He speaks internationally and has published on topics related to EHRs, privacy and security, digital radiology, and patient connectivity. After graduating Magna Cum Laude from Dartmouth College with a degree in Classical Archaeology, and then from the Tufts University School of Medicine, he completed his training in Internal Medicine at Baystate Medical Center, and earned his MPH in Health Policy and Management at the University of Massachusetts at Amherst.

Jerome A. Osheroff, MD, FACP, FACMI, is Chief Clinical Informatics Officer at Thomson Micromedex, where he helps ensure that the company's current and future clinical decision support (CDS) offerings are optimally responsive to healthcare needs. For two decades Dr. Osheroff has been building understanding of clinicians' information needs and helping ensure that information technology is successfully applied to better fulfilling these needs. These efforts include guiding development of commercially successful clinical decision support products, helping healthcare organizations and clinicians use CDS to improve care processes and outcomes, leading research into clinical information management, and helping guide national policy on CDS. Dr. Osheroff is on the medical staff and is Adjunct Assistant Professor of Medicine at the University of Pennsylvania Health System in Philadelphia. He is a fellow of the American College of Physicians and the American College of Medical Informatics and chairs the HIMSS Clinical Decision Support Task Force.

Daniel Z. Sands, MD, MPH, FACMI, is an internationally recognized lecturer, consultant, and thought leader in the area of clinical computing and patient and clinician empowerment through the use of computer technology. In 2004, he became the Chief Medical Officer and Vice President for Clinical Strategies for Zix Corporation. Prior to that, Dr. Sands was the Clinical Systems Integration Architect at Beth Israel Deaconess Medical Center in Boston, where he had worked since 1991. He earned his medical degree at Ohio State University, and a master's degree at Harvard School of Public Health. Dr. Sands did residency training at Boston City Hospital and an informatics fellowship at Beth Israel Deaconess Medical Center. He is an Assistant Professor of Medicine at Harvard Medical School and maintains a primary care practice in which he makes extensive use of health information technology. Dr. Sands is the recipient of numerous health IT awards, sits on the board of the American Medical Informatics Association, and has been elected to the American College of Medical Informatics.

Cheryl Servais, MPH, is Vice President and Compliance and Privacy Officer for Precyse Solutions. Ms. Servais has proven expertise in a wide range of health information management-related areas, including product development and marketing strategies, system analysis and installation, operations improvement and re-engineering, electronic medical record project management, DRG and data quality analysis and education, compliance strategies, and clinical database management. Ms. Servais most recently established HIM Consulting Services, which provided a variety of services to various HIM consulting companies and was also associated with Atlanta-based eWebCoding/InterTech as a consultant and Domain Expert. Prior to that, Ms. Servais held increasingly responsible positions with Tenet Healthcare, ultimately serving as the company's Manager of Health Information Services. Other past experience includes medical records management at three California hospitals and research at UCLA's School of Public Health. Ms. Servais holds a BS in Health Records, and an MPH in Health Information Systems from UCLA.

Janet Stanek, MBA, RHIA, CPHIMS, FHIMSS, is Vice-President & CIO at Stormont-Vail Healthcare, an integrated healthcare delivery system comprised of a 586-bed acute care hospital, 80-bed psychiatric hospital and 130-physician multi-specialty clinic with 19 locations in Northeast Kansas. Ms. Stanek's divisional responsibilities include the information systems, health information management, biomedical engineering, telecommunications and materials management departments. Ms. Stanek had held various management and administrative positions in the healthcare field over the past 20 years. She is a Registered Health Information Administrator, Certified Professional in Healthcare Information & Management Systems, and a Fellow of HIMSS. She serves on the HIMSS Ambulatory Care and Advocacy & Public Policy Steering Committees. For the past several years, Stanek's focus has been on the implementation of electronic medical record systems throughout the organization. Ms. Stanek holds a BS degree from the State University of New York College of Technology, Utica, and an MBA from Alfred University, Alfred, New York.

Kathy J. Westhafer, RHIA, CHPS, is currently the Corporate Director, Health Information Management Services for Christiana Care Health Services located in Wilmington, Delaware. During her tenure there, she has been actively involved in the implementation of a registration system, document imaging system, ambulatory care and inpatient electronic health record systems as well as various departmental systems. She has been an adjust faculty member at the Delaware Technical and Community College and is an active member of the American Health Information Management Association (AHIMA), serving on the e-HIM workgroup on the legal health record and writing for the Journal of AHIMA. In addition, Ms. Westhafer is a member of HIMSS, Pennsylvania Health Information Association (HIMA) and is Past President of the Delaware HIMA.

Patricia B. Wise, RN, MA, MSN, is Vice President, Electronic Health Record (EHR) Initiative for HIMSS and has oversight of the HIMSS Nicholas E. Davies Awards for excellence in EHRs in hospitals, ambulatory practices and public health agencies. Additionally, she leads the Society's work in ambulatory care, studying the challenges of EHR implementation and the return on investment. Prior to joining HIMSS, Col. Wise was on active duty for 28 years with the U.S. Army, serving in a variety of worldwide positions. She is a retired Colonel and former Chief Nurse Executive and Deputy Commander of Eisenhower Army Medical Center in Augusta, GA. While on active duty, Col. Wise was selected for a legislative internship in the office of Senator Daniel Inouye. Following retirement from the Army, Col. Wise joined Computer Based Patient Record Institute-Healthcare Open System and Trials (CPRI-HOST) as Executive Director, a position she remained in until the CPRI-HOST merger with HIMSS in the summer of 2002. Col. Wise received her BSN from Villanova University, and her MSN from University of Maryland. She is a graduate of the US Army War College in Carlisle, Pennsylvania.

Martin L. Zola is Chief Technology Officer at Quality IT Partners with over 25 years of experience in all aspects of IT operations. He specializes in renovating the technical infrastructures of healthcare organizations. Over the past ten years he has designed and implemented online medical record systems including CPRs, EMRs, and EHRs. Mr. Zola takes an enterprise view of architectural issues, striving to ensure that the implemented solution is a balanced blend of functional fulfillment, technical performance, and cost effectiveness. His articles on technical infrastructure have appeared in a variety of technical publications and conference proceedings.

The following individuals contributed case studies or other content for this book:

Terri Andrews, RN, MBA
Clinical Systems Manager
Alamance Regional Medical Center
Burlington, North Carolina

Ted Bailey
CIO/Vice President of Information Systems
Bon Secours
Florida

Lynn Boecler, PharmD, MS
Director of Pharmacy Services
Evanston Hospital
Evanston Northwestern Healthcare
Evanston, Illinois

Jennifer Guite, RN, MS
Senior Systems Analyst, Information Services
Christiana Care Health System
Wilmington, Delaware

John T. Hinton, DO, MPH
Chief Medical Officer
Compass Group, Inc.
Cincinnati, Ohio

David Kane, CPA, MBA
Executive Director
Ogden Clinic
Ogden, Utah

Stanley S. Kent, RPh, MS
Assistant Vice President
Evanston Northwestern Healthcare
Evanston, Illinois

Deborah Kohn, RHIA, CHE, CPHIMS
Principal
Dak Systems Consulting
San Mateo, California

Robert J. Lamberts, MD
Senior Partner
Evans Medical Group
Evans, Georgia

Donnie La Rue
Pharmacy Supervisor
Peninsula Regional Medical Center
Salisbury, Maryland

Stephanie R. Olivier, CPHIMS, MBA
Director, Regional IT Instrastructure
Sutter Health
Sacramento, California

Mary Otto, RN, BSN, MHSA
Manager, Care Provider Systems
Information Services
North Broward Hospital District
Ft. Lauderdale, Florida

Sherry Phillips-Dykes, BS, RN
Senior Clinical Analyst
Forrest General Hospital
Hattiesburg, Mississippi

Kathy Smith, RN, MS
Informatics Nurse Specialist
University of Colorado Hospital
Denver, Colorado

Stephen R. Smith
Chief Information Officer
Hospital of the University of Pennsylvania
Philadelphia, Pennsylvania

Vivienne Smith, RN, BSN
Informatics Nurse Specialist
University of Colorado Hospital
Denver, Colorado

Nancy Grey Stetson, RN, CPHIMS, PMP, FHIMSS
Senior Project Manager, ChartMaxx
MedPlus, Inc., a Quest Diagnostics Company
Alpharetta, Georgia

Lynn Sund, RN, MS, MBA
Vice President, Chief Nurse Executive
Saint Francis Health System
Tulsa, Oklahoma

Brett E. Wallace, MD
Kansas Orthopedics and Sports Medicine, P.A.
Topeka, Kansas

Acknowledgments

I am both inspired by and grateful to the 34 authors and contributors of this book. They reflect the best in HIMSS members: practitioners in healthcare IT who strive for excellence, and who are willing to take the time to share their experiences, both good and bad, with their peers.

This book was initiated by the HIMSS EHR Steering Committee and guided by the EHR Toolkit Task Force. Task force members Barbara Buckheit and Fran Morrison were particularly helpful at making suggestions for the book outline and overall chapter content. Fanny Hawkins, Toby Clark, Cheryl Servais, and Marty Zola provided useful feedback on the structure of the book as well as authored chapters. Richard Epstein, MD, Professor of Anesthesiology at Jefferson Medical College, and David Troiano, RPh, MSIA, Senior Manager at First Consulting Group, provided useful feedback on earlier drafts of the book. Alicia Miller, RPh, MS, Associate Director of Pharmacy, The Ohio State University, reviewed Chapter 6 on the medication process.

I count among my most rewarding experiences as a HIMSS member the opportunity to work with such a competent, energetic and devoted professional staff. For this project I am indebted to Gail Arnett, Program Manager for EHR Initiatives, for keeping us organized and focused as a task force. Fran Perveiler, Vice President of Communications, guided me throughout the development of the book and directed the process of bringing it to publication. Anne Ellis, our copyeditor, improved the quality of our writing, giving our authors/contributors a more consistent voice. Finally, this book would not have come about, like many other EHR endeavors, without the vision and tireless leadership of Pat Wise, Vice President of EHR Initiatives.

I am indebted to many colleagues from Christiana Care Health System who have directly and indirectly supported this effort. Steve Hess, Christiana Care CIO, encouraged me to take on this book and provided me with the flexibility needed to complete it. Lynne McCone, with whom I have collaborated for many years, reviewed the book and offered support throughout. Leo Gilmore, now of Lancaster General Hospital, provided me with the opportunity to lead many of Christiana Care's EHR initiatives, and Elizabeth Schreppler, Joyce Witkowski, Kim Taylor, and Jennifer Guite have mentored me in the complexities and challenges of clinical system implementations. Christine Chastain-Warheit and Ellen Justice of Christiana Care Medical Libraries also provided assistance.

The support of my family has been essential. Jack Riley, my father-in-law and a leader in the quality field, has plied me with valuable insights and a constant supply of reading. My children, Ben and Elizabeth, tolerated, usually with good humor, my obsession with completing this endeavor. My greatest thanks goes to my wife Eileen. Her loving encouragement, patient support, and willingness to spend countless evenings with a physically present but mentally aloof husband made this book possible. She represents the very best that a partner can be and is a blessing that I am thankful for every day.

Joe Miller, Editor

Contents

SECTION IV: IMPLEMENTATION CONSIDERATIONS

Introduction

Joe Miller, MA, FHIMSS

In 1999, the Institute of Medicine (IOM) shocked the American public with its estimate that between 40,000 and 90,000 lives are lost annually due to medical errors. While the IOM provided a balanced view of the causes, many organizations, including the Leapfrog Group, seized on one solution to improve patient safety: computerized provider order entry (CPOE). Healthcare providers across the country rushed to acquire new information systems that promised that errors resulting from poor handwriting and communication would soon be a thing of the past. Six years later, however, estimates suggest that less than 5% of hospitals have implemented CPOE.

The glacial progress of CPOE adoption has many causes, not the least of which are provider resistance and clinical/organizational processes that are enormously difficult to change. Yet in many cases what made adoption of CPOE impractical was a lack of comprehensive, highly reliable, and easily accessible clinical information systems. In other words, healthcare organizations did not have an electronic health record (EHR) that could deliver all the information the provider needs at the time of order entry to ensure that downstream processes in the pharmacy and other departments were coordinated effectively.

The desire to leverage technology to improve patient safety, reduce costs, and improve care—long endorsed by healthcare providers, and more recently championed by government and standards organizations (discussed in Chapter 1)—is creating enormous momentum for the EHR. Yet the obstacles to EHR implementation are as daunting as the benefits are promising. Obstacles include high costs; limited funding; few products that are easy to install, fully functional, and interoperable; and long-entrenched attitudes and healthcare processes that are slow to yield to the opportunities of technology.

The purpose of this book is to offer practical information on the realities of implementing the EHR to information technology (IT) professionals, clinicians, and healthcare leadership. While much has been written about the value and importance of the EHR, and much advice offered on planning, this publication goes a step further to offer detailed information on the implementation of the major components of the EHR.

This is less a book about technology than it is about implementing technology and changing the processes and perspectives of caregivers. The fact is that the initial costs of EHR hardware and software are usually far exceeded (sometimes by a factor of two or three) by the costs of in-house staff and consultant resources needed to implement them. Furthermore, the quality of implementation and the amount of process change

EHR implementation is able to generate drive the benefits realized by the EHR. This book focuses on meeting these challenges of EHR implementation and leaves the more technical discussions to others.

The authors of the following chapters include physicians, nurses, IT professionals, and academicians serving on the front lines of EHR system implementations today. They hail from small to large organizations, community hospitals and teaching facilities, primary care practices and integrated delivery networks. Each brings a hands-on perspective to the challenges and solutions of implementation in his or her area of expertise.

WHAT IS AN ELECTRONIC HEALTH RECORD?

What is an EHR? Figure I-1 provides one of the most widely accepted definitions of the EHR, used in the 2003 Institute on Medicine report titled *Key Capabilities of an Electronic Health Record System*.[1] However, for a more detailed definition, this book

 Longitudinal collection of electronic health information for and about persons, where health information is defined as information pertaining to the health of an individual or healthcare provided to an individual

 Immediate electronic access to person- and population-level information by authorized, and only authorized users

 Provision of knowledge and decision-support that enhance the quality, safety, and efficiency of patient care

 Support of efficient processes for healthcare delivery

Source: Institute of Medicine 2003. Used by permission.

Figure I-1: What Is an Electronic Health Record

uses as its point of reference the Health Level Seven (HL7) standard that was approved in April 2004.[2] This standard will continue to evolve for the foreseeable future. It will have an enormous impact on providers, consultants, and vendors as it becomes the common benchmark of efforts at accreditation, certification, and perhaps ultimately, reimbursement. Moreover, the HL7 EHR standard offers provider organizations a very clear definition of what the EHR is and a yardstick for measuring their progress toward realizing it.

This book views the EHR not necessarily as one single system but as a broad set of functionalities that, depending on the organization, may be provided by one or many systems from one or many vendors. Furthermore, the implementation of the EHR is not a single project but rather a series of initiatives that represent more of a "journey" than a "destination." Most organizations have started their EHR, but since there is no single road map for sequencing EHR functionality, one organization may be approaching order management as its next big project while another is taking on clinical documentation or decision support. Therefore, this book was not designed to be read cover to cover but rather to be "consulted" by chapter as an organization embarks on or enhances its EHR capabilities.

One challenge in preparing this book has been to address the EHR in both acute care and ambulatory settings. These are two very similar and at the same time very different environments. To counter the natural bias toward the acute care setting, two chapters specifically on the ambulatory EHR (Chapters 3 and 11) are included although all chapters contain a wealth of ambulatory setting material.

While each of the chapters is the output of its listed author, we have worked to provide unifying themes throughout the book. Our overarching theme is a focus on implementation challenges and solutions and their impact on clinical processes. Common tables highlight citations documenting benefits (*The Evidence-Based EHR*), the HL7 standard (*The HL7 EHR Prescription*), and future trends (*Three-Year Prognosis*). Finally, 20 case studies illustrate how organizations have approached some of the more challenging issues in EHR implementation.

References

1   Institute of Medicine. *Key Capabilities of an Electronic Health Record System*, 2003.

2   HL7 DSTU.

SECTION I

PLANNING

CHAPTER 1

The Evolving National Agenda for the EHR

Patricia B. Wise, RN, MA, MSN

The promotion of the EHR, long the passion of healthcare technology professionals, has leaped to the forefront of our national agenda in recent years to become a leading public policy issue. From 2003 to 2005 the EHR has been literally "jump-started" through a series of federal and standard-setting initiatives. While the focus of this book is primarily "local"—that is, how the EHR is built one hospital and practice at a time—these initiatives are essential if there is any hope of sharing information beyond the walls of individual provider organizations. This chapter offers an overview of the key players and the evolving national strategies for the EHR.

In 1991, the Institute of Medicine (IOM) released *The Computer-based Patient Record: An Essential Technology for Health Care*, thus beginning an era of struggle as healthcare attempted to move forward and enjoy the gains realized by other business and industry sectors as they embraced the rapidly increasing power of information technology (IT). Since that time numerous efforts across the country have attempted to encourage the adoption, implementation, and use of interoperable electronic health records. Most efforts failed due to a lack of sophisticated systems, inadequate funding, and a paucity of information technology standards. Notable exceptions were a few cutting-edge hospital systems that invested in IT in order to improve efficiency and patient care.[1] Recently, a new movement to automate clinical care and facilitate data sharing is sweeping the nation. This movement focuses on building the infrastructure that will enable the development of the EHR.

Throughout the 1990s a computer-based medical record was referred to as a computerized patient record (CPR), electronic medical record (EMR), and most recently the EHR. Frequently these terms were used synonymously because there was no widely accepted definition or standard that outlined core functions and data elements.

In the spring of 2003, the Centers for Medicare & Medicaid Services (CMS) within the Department of Health and Human Services (HHS) approached the standard development organization Health Level Seven (HL7) to develop a functional model for the EHR (Figure 1-1). CMS intended to use this standard as the basis of a differential reimbursement program, first as pay for use, then as pay for performance.[2] The timeline for this effort was ambitious: an EHR standard by the end of 2003. After two ballots,

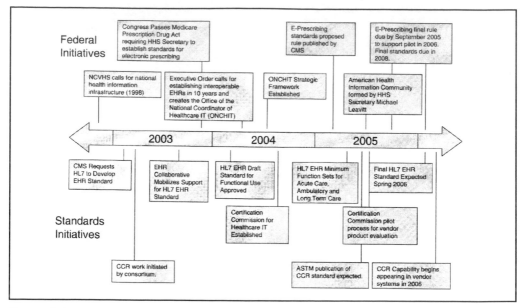

Figure 1-1: EHR Initiatives: The "Jump-Start" Years

and a nationwide process aimed at gathering input and consensus, HL7 produced a draft standard for trial use (DSTU) in 15 months.

Despite the accomplishment of a DSTU, HL7's work has not concluded. Currently under development are minimum function sets (MFS) that will provide more detail regarding the 140 EHR functions found in the DSTU. An MFS for a small to mid-size ambulatory physician practice might contain fewer than 40 functions, approximately half of which are clinical while the rest are related to supportive and infrastructure activity. It is anticipated that MFS will go to ballot in 2005. Along with the minimum function sets, HL7 is also expected to produce conformance statements for each of the multiple functions in an MFS.[2]

While HL7 was working on the EHR Functional Model, the E31 Committee on Healthcare Informatics of ASTM, an American National Standards Institute (ANSI), was preparing the Continuity of Care Record (CCR) for ballot. Now a balloted standard, the CCR is technology- and vendor-neutral and is written in XML that can stand alone or be incorporated into the HL7 Clinical Document Architecture (CDA).

The CCR evolved from a Patient Care Referral Form required by the state of Massachusetts (see Chapter 4 on the assessment process). This paper form was completed by providers whenever there was a transfer of care. The electronic version, the CCR, was designed for provider-to-provider communication as the patient moves from one care setting to another. Not an EHR, the CCR would be completed at the time of the transfer of care or consultation. The CCR is a snapshot of the patient including basic demographics, condition, diagnosis, allergies, medication, plan of care, history, and procedures. The CCR can easily be copied and provided to the patient for incorporation into his or her personal health record.

The ASTM Subcommittee on EHR is expected to finalize a CCR Standard Specification in 2005. If the ballot is affirmative, this XML schema might become a cornerstone of interoperable EHRs.

In April 2004, President Bush officially acknowledged the importance to the federal government of health information technology by issuing an executive order creating the position of a National Health IT Coordinator. Dr. David Brailer was appointed as the first coordinator and tasked with managing programs and policies regarding health IT across the federal government. The president's goal is for all Americans to have an EHR within a decade.[1]

In July 2004, Tommy Thompson, then HHS Secretary, kicked off the Decade of Health Information Technology by announcing a series of steps the federal government would be taking to accelerate adoption of EHR systems, e-prescribing, and other initiatives. Dr. Brailer outlined the strategy with the Framework for Strategic Action (Table 1-1).[3]

Table 1-1: Framework for Strategic Action,
Office of the National Health IT Coordinator

Goal	Features	Strategies
Inform clinical practice	• Centers largely on efforts to bring EHRs directly into clinical practice • Clinicians across the U.S. will have information tools when and where they need them	• Create incentives for EHR adoption • Reduce risk of EHR investment • Promote EHR diffusion in rural and underserved areas
Interconnect clinicians	• Will allow for the secure movement of health information so that EHRs will realize their full benefit • Will allow information to be portable and to move consumers from one point of care to another • Will require an interoperable infrastructure to help clinicians get access to critical health care information when clinical and/or treatment decisions are being made	• Foster regional collaborations • Develop a national health information network • Coordinate federal health information systems
Personalize care	• Consumer-centric information helps individuals have choice, control and the ability to manage their own wellness and assists with their personal health care decisions	• Encourage use of personal health records • Enhance informed consumer choice • Promote use of telehealth systems
Improve population health	• Population health improvement requires the collection of timely, accurate, and detailed clinical information • Population health also requires the reporting of critical findings to public health officials, clinical trials and other research, and feedback to clinicians	• Unify public health surveillance architectures • Streamline quality and health status monitoring • Accelerate research and dissemination of evidence

Significantly, both CMS and private payers continue to indicate their intent to provide incentives for use of EHR systems and the electronic reporting of quality data. This move to "pay for performance" is being targeted at physician practices, providing there is a mechanism to ensure the EHR and related technologies are robust enough to deliver the anticipated benefits. Providers meanwhile are being faced with a dazzling array of products and a great degree of uncertainty regarding product suitability, quality, interoperability, and data portability.

In response to provider concerns and one of the major recommendations emerging from the Office of the National Coordinator for Healthcare Information Technology (ONCHIT), three healthcare associations, including the Healthcare Information and Management Systems Society (HIMSS), launched the Certification Commission for Healthcare Information Technology (CCHIT). The Commission's purpose is to create an efficient, credible, sustainable mechanism for the certification of healthcare information technology products. This certification process will help to reduce the risk of IT investment by providers and to ensure interoperability of IT products with the emerging local and national health information infrastructures. The Commission will focus its initial efforts on IT market sectors expected to enjoy the greatest potential acceleration of adoption from product certification. A consensus has emerged, supported by Dr. Brailer's report, that EHRs marketed to the physician office practice represent the most appropriate place to start. The Commission will define a minimum set of functions that will certify whether or not a vendor product can be considered an ambulatory product. Initial certification requirements and processes for testing are scheduled to be in place by late summer 2005.

As the nation moves forward toward adoption of EHRs, the ability to increase the quality and efficiency of care is greatly enhanced if healthcare information can be exchanged both on regional and national levels. ONCHIT's *Framework for Strategic Action* outlines a national vision for a health information exchange. This exchange depends on the development of regional health information organizations (RHIOs) throughout the nation. Communities in all states can facilitate the adoption of interoperable EHRs by developing RHIOs that are intended to promote the sharing of clinical information (see Chapter 10).

The RHIO model is based on the adoption of consistent, technically sound interoperability standards. To that end, Dr. Brailer published a request for information (RFI) in November 2004. The RFI sought information for developing a national health information network (NHIN) to facilitate the exchange of data between interoperable EHRs. A common theme from the over 500 responses to the RFI was the need for a stronger federal role in guiding the many initiatives to establish standards for interoperability.

Toward this end, HHS Secretary Michael Leavitt announced in June 2005 the formation of the American Health Information Community (AHIC). The AHIC is a public-private advisory commission, chaired by Secretary Leavitt, that will focus on making recommendations in four areas:

- Privacy and security;
- Identification of HIT capabilities that will provide immediate benefits to consumers of healthcare (e.g., drug safety, lab results, bioterrorism surveillance, etc.);

- Creation of a private-sector, consensus-based, standard-setting and harmonization process, and a separate product certification process; and
- Establishment of a nationwide architecture that uses the Internet to share health information in a secure and timely manner.

In addition, HHS funded four Request for Proposals to advance design and technical work on standards harmonization, product certification, NHIN architecture, and privacy and security for health data exchange.

Another federal initiative that deserves mention relates to e-prescribing. In 2003 Congress passed and President Bush signed the Medicare Prescription Drug Improvement and Modernization Act of 2003, which is best known for expanding prescription drug benefits to Medicare beneficiaries. A less prominent component of the act requires that all e-prescriptions offered under the program meet federally established standards. Given the size of the Medicare program, these standards for e-prescribing are expected to become the de facto standards for the industry. In February, 2005 CMS issued a proposed rule specifying an initial set of standards in preparation for a pilot project expected to begin in 2006. Complete, final standards are due in 2008.

EHRs and the providers who use them to enhance the quality of patient care have entered into a tumultuous decade. Rewards will await those who work to integrate the technology into their practice. Providers cannot afford to mimic the ostrich that, with its head in the sand, hopes all will pass by. EHRs are a technology whose time has come.

References

1   The Advisory Board Company. *A National Infrastructure for Health Information Technology.* 2004.

2   HIMSS Standard Insight. December 2004. www.himss.org.

3   HIMSS Standard Insight. September 2004. www.himss.org.

CHAPTER 2

Planning the EHR

Joe Miller, MA, FHIMSS

Acute care providers who are hearing the recent clarion call for the EHR may wonder what it is that they have been working on for the past 10 to 20 years if it was not an EHR. The fact is that while most providers are well down the road to implementing an EHR, few have implemented one that is comprehensive both in functionality and adoption in all areas of the organization. This chapter suggests how an organization can conduct an EHR "self-assessment" and highlights several critical success factors in EHR planning. (EHR planning issues unique to the ambulatory EHR environment are discussed in Chapter 3.)

Conducting an EHR self-assessment using the HL7 EHR standard is an important step for defining or refining an organization's EHR plan. As noted in Chapter 1, current efforts by federal agencies and other organizations are positioning the standard as the metric for "certifying" EHR systems among vendors. Providers would do well to determine their EHR strengths and weaknesses now. This chapter highlights three critical success factors for EHR implementation: clarity of vision, stakeholder commitment, and effective project management.

CONDUCTING THE SELF-ASSESSMENT

If an organization has not arrived at the "destination" of the EHR, how far away is it from this goal? The HL7 EHR standard provides the best yardstick against which to measure an organization's progress toward implementing the EHR. With 140 functions,

---

Contributors to this chapter include Martin L. Zola (EHR visioning), John T. Hinton, DO, MPH (stakeholder alignment), and Nancy Grey Stetson, RN, CPHIMS, PMP, FHIMSS (project management). Stephanie R. Olivier, CPHIMS, MBA, contributed Case Study 1 on Managing the EHR Project Portfolio.

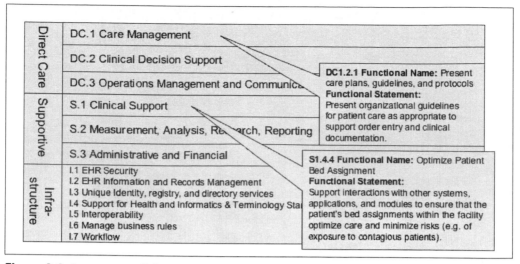

Figure 2-1: Structure of the HL7 EHR Standard

the standard is sufficiently comprehensive and detailed for an organization to conduct an initial self-assessment of where it stands in implementing its EHR.

Figure 2-1 provides the HL7 standard's basic structure. As shown, there are three major categories (Direct Care, Supportive, and Infrastructure) that are then divided into 13 sub-categories. These then contain 140 "functional statements" including detailed descriptions of the function. Upcoming versions of the standard will define a Minimum Function Sets (MFSs) for each care setting (acute, ambulatory, long term care, community). These MFSs will designate each functional descriptor as "essential now," "essential future" or "optional." For example, the MFS for large acute care organizations might designate the function "Support for Standard Assessments" (DC2.1.1) as "essential now" but for a small ambulatory practice it is "essential future" and for long term care it is "optional."

The EHR self-assessment for providers should examine the organization's progress for each functional statement considering both the capability and the scope of the implementation.

Capability

Capability is the extent to which the function features have been implemented. For example, an organization may be using an online assessment form at intake that has minimal prompts to guide the assessor (see functional descriptor DC 2.1.1). This would be considered a lower level of capability or conformance than an online assessment that uses prompts to guide the assessor to acquire specific information.

Scope/Penetration

Scope is the extent to which the implementation is complete throughout the organization. For example, an organization may be using an online assessment form for patients directly admitted to medical-surgical units but not for other patients such as those admitted for surgery.

Table 2-1 provides an example of how a provider organization that includes a hospital and a number of physician practices might assess its conformance with three functions that fall within the Direct Care section of the standard. In this example, the hospital site has not implemented a problem list and thus has categorized itself as "Low." The physician practices have available a fully functional problem list (capability was rated "High") but there are several specialty practices that are not currently using it, so the scope of implementation was rated "Medium." While there are no strict or established methods for conducting a self-assessment, a process that considers both capability and scope for each of the functions will assist an organization in exposing its "EHR gap" and its opportunities for future EHR development.

Table 2-1: Sample EHR Self-Assessment

HL7 EHR Function	Hospital Capability	Hospital Scope	Practice Capability	Practice Scope
DC1.1.3.2 Manage problem list	Low	Low	High	Medium
DC1.1.3.2 Manage medication list	Medium	High	High	Medium
DC1.1.3.2 Manage allergy and adverse reaction list	High	High	High	Medium

CREATING/UPDATING YOUR EHR PLAN

Closing the "EHR gap" is the focus of the EHR plan. An organization's EHR plan should specify the series of initiatives that will move the organization toward a more complete realization of its EHR. But establishing when and how an organization goes about working each initiative is likely to have less to do with the HL7 standard than with the organization's broader business needs and capacity. Among the factors to be considered in setting EHR priorities are business alignment, organizational capacity, infrastructure, and the inter-dependence of the EHR projects.

Business Alignment

Does the function align with a business priority of the organization? EHR initiatives are only as valuable as the tactical or strategic business need that they satisfy. While EHR initiatives are often costly to implement, unless they are aligned with the organization's business priorities they are unlikely to receive the resources required to implement them properly.

Organizational Capacity

Does the organization have the capacity (e.g., staffing, focus, change tolerance) to implement the function? Implementing an electronic medication administration record is an enormous change to nursing process and requires extensive training. Implementing this while nursing resources are being tapped for other major initiatives diminishes the likelihood of success.

Infrastructure

Is the current IT infrastructure capable of supporting the next phase of EHR initiatives? Busy caregivers require that EHR components will be implemented on systems that are reliable, have good performance, and can be quickly recovered. If the infrastructure is not capable of providing the level of availability demanded by the users, then the initiative should be deferred.

Interdependence

What are the interdependencies that must be considered? Interdependencies can be both technical and functional. Technical interdependencies might be related to the need to replace a legacy and difficult-to-interface pharmacy system before beginning a computerized provider order entry system. A functional inter-dependence might be the need to implement point-of-care testing before point-of-care documentation to ensure that the nurse's workflow does not become fragmented.

The final step is establishing the plan for future development of the EHR. The EHR plan is likely to be part of the organization's overall information technology plan that would include administrative and other systems. The key to the EHR component is that it reflects a sequential approach toward meeting both the organization's goals and the goal of compliance with the HL7 EHR standard. Three critical success factors stand out when executing the EHR plan: clarity of vision, trueness of stakeholder alignment, and quality of project management.

CRITICAL SUCCESS FACTOR: CREATING THE VISION

An EHR vision is a vivid description of how an EHR will function in a particular healthcare environment and how it will improve patient care and operations. The vision is an idealistic description of how the implemented technologies will improve the care delivery environment. It should draw the interest and attention of as wide an audience as possible. If composed properly, it will be motivating to those affected by its implementation.

Typically, a documented vision is short in length (two to three pages) and consists of
• A brief description of the problem or opportunity;
• The EHR solution;
• Business and mission justification for the solution;
• Measures of success; and
• Implementation considerations.
The best visions are short and inspiring, enabling the reader to understand how the EHR will benefit the organization.

It is never too late to develop or revive an EHR vision. The key EHR stakeholders should participate in formulating it and the decision makers and the individual responsible for implementation should approve its final draft.

Going forward, project advocates and implementers should articulate the vision often. This judicious repetition of the common goal is important in keeping the organization focused. When properly communicated, the vision helps to ensure that everyone is moving in the same direction and cooperating on decisions based upon a mutual understanding of a common goal.

CRITICAL SUCCESS FACTOR: STAKEHOLDER ALIGNMENT

The Greek scientist Archimedes is quoted as saying, "Give me a lever long enough and I will move the world." Achieving stakeholder alignment will provide the lever to achieve successful implementation, desired behavior change, and positive outcomes for the EHR. The rollout of any new process or tool in healthcare can produce ripples of excitement, anticipation, and/or fear. This is especially true for the EHR. Alignment of stakeholders creates the necessary support structure and sustains the momentum necessary to accomplish the initiative.

Successful technology implementation and adoption requires identification of critical resources, understanding the configuration of participants, and clarity around the work to be accomplished. Alignment assures the project's responsiveness to the current environment and individuals who have an investment in the process.

Each step in planning, purchasing, installing, and implementing the EHR must address the impact on each stakeholder. Although physicians, nurses, pharmacists and IT specialists play prominent roles in the project, active participation of other clinical and non-clinical individuals should be included. Some of the best ideas and sensitivity to the project's potential may come from individuals at the sharp end of the process such as unit clerks or from patients as recipients of clinical services.

Capturing the energy of health care organizations and its employees in the following key dimensions will help achieve the critical success factor of alignment:

- *Motivation:* Change is often resisted, and as described above the vision needs to be inspirational, e.g., it will improve patient safety, productivity, efficiency or cost effectiveness. Sustaining motivation requires continuous competency development of all stakeholders.
- *Process:* Identify the "connectedness" of stakeholders and develop a shared understanding of relationships.
- *Dialogue:* Engaging stakeholders in ongoing conversation and active participation in the project, as well as continuous two-way communication, are essential for sustaining alignment.
- *Results:* Sharing measures of success and opportunities for further action is also crucial. Reporting measures keeps the project focused and fosters performance accountability rather than just documenting activity.

To achieve alignment it is essential to be able to create a shared context for the project. Technology has a way of seducing participants with the marvels of automation and concealing its complexity. The project's goals and purpose need sufficient clarity and detail to demonstrate respect for each constituent and value to their function in the organization. The reward of a successful EHR implementation is not only in the efficiency and effectiveness it brings to patient care but also how its implementation can strengthen the care delivery process and stakeholder relationships.

CRITICAL SUCCESS FACTOR: PROJECT MANAGEMENT

The Project Management Institute (PMI) defines the project management process groups of initiating, planning, executing, monitoring and controlling, and closing as being required for any project.[1] Healthcare project management itself is a challenge, but with the added complexity of an EHR implementation, a solid project management process across all phases of the implementation is critical. Today many healthcare IT departments are establishing project management offices (PMOs) to establish processes within their organization to support and monitor adherence to the PMI process groups. This section discusses these process groups in the context of how they apply to the implementation of an EHR. Since most EHR implementations involve multiple projects, these steps would be repeated for each project. One organization's commitment and approach to the management of its portfolio of EHR projects is highlighted in Case Study 1 at the end of this chapter.

Initiating

The major output of initiation is the Project Charter, which formally authorizes the project and generally sets its scope. In healthcare projects, the project manager and the project team (for both the vendor and the healthcare organization) are typically not involved in the development of the Charter, but rather receive the information once the project has been authorized. It is useful to distribute an Executive Summary to the project managers and their respective steering committees and teams. The Executive Summary is a document that for a given date affords a manager or supervisor perspective at a glance on where project resources will be expended. It assumes a shared project management responsibility between the vendor and the organization. This information is an invaluable aspect of the actual project plan. The Executive Summary briefly describes:

- *Project Charter:* A brief statement of the project scope.
- *Milestones:* Include revenue (hardware, software installation) and project milestones (training, projected go-lives).
- *Implementation time line:* Broken into the projected phases of the implementation.
- *Implementation completion terminology:* This will set the parameters of the project completion at the very beginning of the project.
- *Customer and vendor project teams.*
- *Communications plan:* To clearly delineate the communication format, responsibility, distribution, and frequency.
- *Project risk management:* To define perceived risk at the beginning of the project.
- *Authorizations:* To define responsibility for signoffs (interfaces, installation) and to designate the vendor (if applicable) and organization project manager.
- *Signoff:* The final Executive Summary needs to be signed off by both the customer and the vendor project managers and formally presented to the respective steering committees.

Planning

Planning is more than generating a project plan; in fact, that is the end result of the planning process. The complexity of the EHR initiative—multiple phases, systems, teams, even projects—makes planning an extremely critical process. A tool that can be developed from the Executive Summary is a Phases document. This is a relatively high-level document in table or spreadsheet format that outlines each project phase and then lists tasks and activities that will lead to the project goals for that phase. This one sheet will demonstrate the level of effort across phases and serve as the basis for the Work Breakdown Structure and the project plan.

Executing

One of the biggest challenges in an EHR project is in securing the necessary resources to carry out the project plan. This is where all the planning pays off. The planning process identifies the budget and the project team needs. Because the EHR comprises many different systems and processes, multiple project teams may be required for any given initiative or phase of the implementation. EHR project teams will more than likely be composed of members from different departments, with different IT and clinical areas with different reporting structures.

A critical path in the EHR project portfolio is working with the team members to ensure that their roles and responsibilities are clearly understood. Additionally, how the teams work together, including both vendor and organization teams, is also a critical success factor. Whether there is a PMO that oversees the team(s) or whether one project manager has this job, the teams have to know where they are going and how they are doing. For virtual teams, additional effort needs to be exerted to share information regularly and to schedule routine education and process review meetings. Use the project plan to drive the agenda for these status meetings—add due dates and responsible parties as part of the agenda items. This enables team members to maintain focus and improve productivity as they know that they will be expected to give their status on a given task.

Matrix organizational management skills are essential in an initiative as large as an EHR implementation. By virtue of the Project Charter, project managers are empowered to garner resources to complete the project. This means planning and negotiating with functional managers for the necessary resources—primarily personnel—that need to be in place to fulfill project milestones. One of the best (although sometimes hardest) ways to promote cooperation for resources is to ensure that there is open, two-way communication between the project manager and the functional manager.

Monitoring and Controlling

A change control process is an absolute must in any successful process. Without a defined methodology to monitor deviation from the plan and take corrective action, including obtaining approval for any changes to the plan, the project is susceptible to out-of-control scope creep.

Closure

The biggest caution here is not to wait until the end of the project to document lessons learned. The EHR implementation is huge, with various phases and projects within projects that are interdependent. No single project manager—or even a group of project managers or a PMO—can adequately remember the "gotchas" at the end of the project.

Case Study 1: Managing the EHR Project Portfolio

Organization:	Sutter Health, Northern California
Acute Care Facilities:	28
Staffed Beds:	5,000

Sutter Health is a not-for-profit, integrated delivery system that has made a significant commitment to the use of technology in enhancing patient care. It was the first provider organization on the West Coast to provide 24/7 remote monitoring of patient ICU beds in multiple hospital locations. Another significant patient safety initiative has been the implementation of bedside medication administration using bar coding technology to avoid medication errors. Sutter also recently announced a $150 million investment over two years to implement an integrated inpatient and outpatient EHR. All of these clinical projects fall into an enterprise-wide, formal set of initiatives to improve patient care delivery.

In order to manage the growing number of strategic IT initiatives, Sutter has invested time and money in evaluating enterprise portfolio management (EPM) tools to provide a better mechanism for approving and tracking these complex projects. Enterprise portfolio management is gaining recognition in healthcare industry decision-making for guiding and monitoring the broad array of large and small projects underway within healthcare organizations.

While all organizations use some form of project management for individual projects, EPM is a methodology that allows the coordination of multiple IT projects. Any organization faces the challenge of competing priorities, resource demands, and pressures for cost containment while still being asked to deliver the technological solutions that will, at a minimum, keep the operations running productively and, at best, support organizational transformation. EPM facilitates the necessary coordination and management. It is a means to view the portfolio of projects, much like the asset allocation view of mutual funds, bonds and stocks in a retirement portfolio, and to confirm that objectives, value, risk, and expected outcomes are aligned. EPM balances the subjective assessments of projects with quantifiable objective measurements; applied consistently, it provides executives and IT leadership a tool for monitoring and decision-making.

An important first step for Sutter was to solicit the assistance of an EPM vendor to assess the current level of project portfolio management maturity[2] and to make recommendations for the stages of growth Sutter should strive for in improving project management outcomes. Sutter's assessed level was consistent with what is reported in general for organizations, which is in the range of I to II.[3] The vendor study also helped focus the areas of potential improvement using EPM, predicting the estimated cost savings would be approximately 12% in the first year after implementation. Of the first year savings, 76% was expected to be recognized through an improvement in resource utilization, another 12% through an improvement in project selection and prioritization, and 9% through an improvement in project execution.

An organization must evaluate and prioritize many modules during the selection and implementation phases of an EPM software toolset. Time tracking and integration with the payroll system are high priorities for Sutter. In addition, budget management and enterprise dashboards are important, particularly in monitoring multiple, related EHR projects across geographical regions, such as bandwidth upgrades and ancillary system replacements with Sutter standards.

All of these capabilities are key when approaching a large-scale implementation project such as EHR. Sutter is currently designing the organizational project structure for the EHR rollout and defining the multiple, concurrent projects. Meanwhile, other important operational initiatives must be supported. The use of project portfolio management is viewed as a key element in managing the complexity of an EHR initiative while maintaining the right mix of operational and strategic projects to ensure ultimate success.

References

1 *A Guide to the Project Management Body of Knowledge (PMBOK® Guide), Third Edition.* Newton Square, PA: Project Management Institute; 2004, p 384.

2 Organizational Project Management Maturity Model (OPM3). Project Management Institute; PMI North American Congress; 2003.

3 Project Portfolio Management—A Benchmark of Current Business Practices. Center for Business Practices, Research Offerings. http://www.cbponline.com/Research/PPM%20News.pdf.

CHAPTER 3

Acquiring the Ambulatory EHR

Janet Stanek, MBA, RHIA, CPHIMS, FHIMSS

While the acute care and ambulatory care EHR share much common functionality, the approach for implementing them is often quite different. Acute care EHRs are developed incrementally, literally over decades, with many vendors. Ambulatory EHRs are implemented more quickly and are more likely to rely on a single vendor product. Recognizing these differences, this chapter focuses on the unique features of acquiring and planning for an ambulatory EHR; its companion, Chapter 11, discusses implementation.

When initially considering an EHR, ambulatory practices—which in this context include primary care, specialty (e.g., cardiology, orthopedics), and clinic practices—need to consider what are the most important factors driving their decision. Before the practice leadership leaps to conclusions about software, hardware, and network, they should carefully focus on how the EHR will affect practitioners, office support staff, and overall clinical workflow: What will be the impact on patients, consultants, and others who interact with the practice? Most importantly, what is the overall business strategy that is driving the decision, and what strategies are required to better ensure physician buy-in, with a realistic implementation and use plan in place?[1] While the, size, and complexity of the ambulatory EHR acquisition is different than in the acute care setting, the attention to vision, goals, and clarity of purpose is no less critical to the implementation's success.

USER INVOLVEMENT

User involvement in the planning and selection process will vary depending on the size of the practice, its structure, and whether it is part of a larger integrated delivery

---

Brett E. Wallace, MD, contributed Case Study 2 on Early Experience Drives Integrated EHR Solution.

network. For example, a practice that is associated with a large healthcare institution will typically have a hierarchical decision-making process for an EHR selection that ties into the overall IT strategic plan. A smaller, independent practice is more likely driven by a visionary, such as the practice manager. In either case, user involvement (users defined as those who will be affected by the EHR) in the planning process is critical to ensure that an appropriate system is selected. The legitimacy of the decision is less likely to be questioned during more difficult stages of implementation if participation has been reasonably broad and the reasons for the decision have been documented.

In smaller practices, while decision-making is likely to be limited to a few key individuals, it is nonetheless important for frequent communications about the selection process to occur. These practices typically have staff members who "wear multiple hats" and have developed workflows that enable them to balance multiple demands. They and other users will be well aware that the EHR will be a catalyst for change in the practice and that their work processes will change as a result.

Larger practices should consider establishing an EHR Steering Committee to keep the planning process on track. This committee should (a) have a clearly defined and communicated mission statement, (b) be multidisciplinary, and (c) be sized appropriately to the practice. The committee can be tasked with setting ground rules and guidelines for decision-making. The establishment of this important process cannot be overlooked. For practices associated with a larger healthcare institution, clear leadership of this committee should be established and the membership should include those users who will be "sneezers": people who have influence and spread ideas. Ideally, the membership will be weighted toward thought-leaders in their markets who have the power to spread the word about the goals and get people to listen.[2]

Regardless of what structure is put in place, there will be holdouts (nonconformists, naysayers) who will resist efforts to move to an EHR. Yet without a clear and legitimate structure for communication and decision-making, a practice may be faced with a level of resistance that, if left unchecked, will unduly delay implementation. In the worst-case scenario, this resistance will undermine coming to a decision at all. This will be the case particularly for practices that include specialties such as pediatrics, oncology, infusion centers, and the like. Leaving out any potential user area from the selection process creates additional risk for the project.

A clear understanding of user needs is imperative to the acquisition process. This can be done by the simple steps of shadowing and interviewing how each level of user (nurse, physician, support staff) processes the paper medical record. The more complete the documentation of these processes, using flow-charting or narrative descriptions, the more complete the list of requirements that can be developed. A comprehensive set of requirements will both enable vendors to better respond to the practice's request for information and enable the practice to better evaluate its response.

How well a vendor listens and assists with determining needs prior to acquisition is a strong indicator of how well they will provide support once the product is installed. The EHR is not always a one-size-fits-all proposition. Carefully listening to all users and what their needs are will be important prior to acquisition. Gathering this critical information will also better ensure that the practice will come to the right decision on the selection of the EHR. Table 3-1 outlines examples of user involvement.

Table 3-1: User Involvement in EHR Product Acquisition

Facility Type	Small	Medium	Large or Associated with IDN
Project lead/liaison	X	X	X
Steering committee		X	X
Weekly update meetings		X	X
Executive sponsorship			X
Budget planning	X	X	X
Review and plotting of workflow	X	X	X
Request for information	X	X	X
Request for proposal		X	X

ACQUISITION STRATEGY

The decision to acquire an EHR for many practices is derived from the experience and use of a practice management system. Most practices today have an automated billing system. For small practices this could be a stand-alone server; for medium to large practices, it could be a host server connected to other computers or clients. Some systems also have a patient scheduling system incorporated into their practice management system that shares the same database of basic patient information. This can provide the core foundation for the future EHR strategy.

The move to a single vendor, or clustered, model will lead to a single patient demographic database and easy access from one screen to another. Data and workflow functionality are important considerations in the selection process. Considerations for making the decision to select a solution that is part of an organization's existing vendor's suite of products may include (a) integration of data, (b) ease of use, and (c) features and functionality that meet user requirements. Ultimately, the EHR should improve patient care. The rest of the benefits will follow.

The size and type of practice plays a major role in the type of EHR that is acquired. The acquisition process may be more simplified in a specialty practice than in a multi-specialty practice. More challenges exist in a multi-specialty practice because the EHR will have to meet the needs of all practices, and getting consensus on the best product for all may result in a compromise for some.

When considering the acquisition of an EHR, the practice should assess whether the potential vendor will be able to augment any EHR components that are already in place. This may lead to cost savings and an improved return on investment for the EHR components that a practice has already invested in.

Funding an EHR investment is obviously a huge consideration prior to acquisition. Depending on the size of the practice, capitalizing the investment is a typical funding methodology. Although this may require a significant investment on the acquisition's front end, capitalizing the EHR can provide a depreciation expense, which can be used to fund future capital investments in the practice. The number of years that can be depreciated will, of course, depend on the estimated life-cycle of the EHR solution.

Leasing may be an attractive option if a practice does not have readily available capital dollars to invest. In all cases, hardware can be leased and is typically not tied to the overall EHR contract. Leasing software may also be an option. Some vendors offer what is known as an application service provider (ASP) model. In this case, the vendor provides the practice with both the server hardware and software at a monthly or annual fee. The server(s) can reside at the vendor's location or at the practice location. Practice size will impact the decision as to whether or not the ASP model is a practical funding methodology.

Regardless of the funding mechanism used to acquire the EHR, assessing total ownership cost (TOC) over the life of the EHR contract is imperative. Considerations here include, at a minimum, hardware, software, training, implementation services, future software and hardware upgrades, and support personnel to manage the EHR.

Information Resources for EHR Products

Many resources are readily available for locating the latest information on EHR products, including vendor-specific overviews, product overviews, rankings, and emerging technologies. Key resources are provided in Table 3-2.

Table 3-2: Independent Sources of EHR Product Information

Organization	Web Site
American Health Information Management Association (AHIMA)	www.ahima.org
American Academy of Family Physicians	www.aafp.org
KLAS	www.healthcomputing.com
Gartner Group	www.gartner.com
Healthcare Information and Management Systems Society (HIMSS)	www.HIMSS.org Analytics Ambulatory Care Sector Annual Conference
MD Buyline	www.Mdbuyline.com
Medical Group Management Association (MGMA)	www.mgma.com

PREPARING TO WORK WITH EHR VENDORS

When considering the acquisition of an EHR, it is important to obtain some basic facts about each vendor being considered (Table 3-3). The vendor's qualifications and experience will have an impact on the EHR implementation. The magnitude of this undertaking cannot be overemphasized. Therefore, it is imperative that the practice develop a comfort level with the vendor and those vendor employees that your practice will be interfacing with up front. It is strongly recommended that reference checks, and if possible a site visit, be conducted prior to contract execution.

Table 3-3: Vendor Checklist

☑ Size and composition of the company
☑ Number of products offered and number of installs
☑ Qualifications of all positions within the company
☑ Whether or not they are privately or publicly held and sales history
☑ Company leadership structure

Having a thorough understanding of what will occur once the contract is executed is another important consideration prior to acquisition. The friendly, easily accessible sales executive may not be seen or heard from again, so all commitments made by the vendor should be well documented. It is important that there be an appropriate hand-off so that expectations set for the implementation during the contract negotiation are understood and carried out.

Establishing face-to-face communications with vendor key players is important early in the process. This is one way to begin the process of establishing mutual expectations in writing prior to contract presentation.

Financial negotiations should consider the total cost of ownership. The most intense negotiations often surround the initial cost of hardware and software, when in fact it is often the implementation fees and ongoing annual maintenance costs that constitute the greatest expense.

It is strongly recommended that contracts be reviewed in detail from technical, medical, and legal perspectives prior to execution. It is also beneficial that practice leadership and other key players in the organization be given a summary review of the key terms that are being agreed to prior to execution. Examples of these key terms include support escalation procedure, penalty fees, and vendor expectations of the client.

VENDOR DEMONSTRATIONS

Vendor presentations and interactive Web-based demonstrations (demos) are typical venues for product review. Consideration should be given to the following:

- How do the timing of the demo and the timing of the desired acquisition coincide? If the spread is too great, a re-demo of the product is recommended.
- Determine the level of demo that is appropriate based on the target audience. Physicians may benefit from the 30,000-feet-level demo initially, whereas the practice leadership will require a detailed demo.
- Being aware of what components of the product demo are currently available features and functionalities, versus which ones are in development and will be available in the future (typically known as vaporware), is imperative to understanding the product.
- Site visits are recommended but only after narrowing the competition down to one or two vendors. Having the right mix of staff attend the site visit will better guarantee a clear understanding of all aspects of the product and what goes along with implementing and managing the solution long term.

CONDUCTING A SUCCESSFUL COMPETITIVE VENDOR PROCUREMENT

There are benefits to narrowing down vendor options in order to focus on the acquisition of the EHR and not waste too much time on a multitude of vendor visits. As noted previously, there are numerous resources available to assist with vendor and product research. Conducting a request for proposal (RFP) can help with the narrowing process. Depending on the size of the practice, an outside firm may be engaged to assist with this. A request for information (RFI) is another option for narrowing the search for a vendor. This is a slimmed-down version of an RFP that may better serve your needs if resources are not available to do a detailed requirements specification.

Establishing and maintaining an internal focal contact point for vendor discussions is important prior to any serious negotiations. If too many parties get involved, the vendor may not get a clear understanding of what the needs are and design a contract that will not produce the desired outcome.

Both the vendor and customer have equal accountability for the implementation's success. Before committing to an implementation schedule, it is important to give careful consideration to what practice resources will be needed during and after implementation. The vendor should be able to articulate its expectations as to which practice resources are required for how long and when.

Table 3-4 provides an overview of the complete acquisition process.

Table 3-4: **Timeline for EHR System Selection for Large Ambulatory Practice**

Task	Month 1	2	3	4	5	6	7	8	9	10	11	12
Identify EHR drivers	■											
Identify anticipated barriers		■										
Identify leadership	■											
Establish EHR steering committee		■										
Identify funding source			■									
Research EHR products			■									
Consider RFP or RFI				■								
Attend a trade show		■	■	■								
Narrow selection to top 3 vendors						■						
Conduct product demonstrations							■					
Determine if user and price requirements are met								■				
Attend a site visit to a similar user									■			
Obtain final contract and pricing proposal from selected vendor										■		
Negotiate contract											■	
Execute contract												■

READY FOR IMPLEMENTATION

This chapter has discussed a number of key considerations that need to be taken into account during the planning and acquisition phases. An organization is ready for implementation (see Chapter 11) if the following exist:

1. Vendor is selected.
2. Contract is executed.
3. Point person or steering committee is established.
4. Hardware and software have been installed.
5. Training is underway or is completed.

Case Study 2: Early Experience Drives Integrated EHR Solution

Organization:	Kansas Orthopedic & Sports Medicine Clinic (KOSM), Topeka, Kansas
Facilities:	1
Visits:	19,000
Type:	Specialty Ambulatory Practice

After years of shuffling paper medical records between offices, KOSM had two objectives when the organization decided to invest in an EHR:

- To streamline the billing and patient information processing, and
- To be interconnected and prepared for the eventuality of the digital age, including digital documentation as well as imaging.

In 1995, KOSM added a small information system that stored patient notes and other clinical results. This served as the building block for an EHR. With only three workstations and one printer in its two-story clinic, KOSM quickly realized that access to the information was not adequate. Information needed to be readily retrievable electronically, not only for the patient care but for other requesting parties such as insurers and attorneys.

Drawing on its experience with automation and the rapid improvements with technology overall, KOSM realized the potential an EHR could have on its practice, both from patient care and efficiency perspectives. In 1999, the organization set out to acquire a fully integrated practice management and EHR solution.

KOSM took the following into consideration prior to investing in the integrated solution:

- Based on incremental experience, KOSM concluded that it needed to invest in a more expensive solution than originally planned in order to achieve its vision. Facing some resistance, all partners needed to be convinced that the time and money involved in the EHR investment were worth the effort. Cash outlay remained a concern.
- KOSM required a tightly integrated practice management and EHR solution.
- The need to get educated on basic IT principles and server capabilities and long-term management of the solution was paramount. Most of this education was achieved through independent study as well as attendance at the American Academy of Orthopedic Surgeons' annual meeting, where EHR vendors were present.

- KOSM needed to decide between purchasing a new system from its existing vendor or moving to a new solution provider. Of significant consideration was how big the change would be for the existing users in the practice, including support personnel.
- The type of platform and devices that would be the most efficient and accepted for the entire practice in order to achieve adoption of the EHR solution was another key consideration.

After interviewing providers in the practice, KOSM issued an RFP to various vendors identifying their requirements. Vendor selection occurred quickly because KOSM decided to purchase a new system from its existing vendor.

Lessons learned and considerations that were missed prior to acquisition included:

- Scrutinize the contract so that a practice does not over-purchase. An example of this would be purchasing a maintenance agreement on hardware through the software vendor that is already included as part of the hardware vendor's agreement.
- Determine the scope of your implementation plan prior to acquisition based on your practice. For example, entering key clinical data prior to adopting full template-based documentation may be the preferred route rather than overwhelming users.
- Don't delay the decision to purchase a system based on the fact that technology costs may go down in the next 2 years. Your needs and your vision should be considered first. Keep in mind what led you to look for a solution in the first place.
- Set up the system with thin client devices (see Chapter 13). Benefits include the overall management of the system as well providing you with a more secure solution.
- Determine up front how to initially combine the old paper medical record components with your EHR solution.
- Determine the infrastructure and device needs prior to implementation based on practice workflow. KOSM required a significant upgrade of their network infrastructure as well as an increase in the number of printers that would be required.
- Develop a centralized backup solution that is managed on a daily basis.
- Develop and publish a comprehensive computer use policy and post where it is accessible to all users.
- Consider developing an intranet for your practice to keep the lines of communication open.

Today, KOSM has a successful EHR model in place with some remaining paper, which is incorporated manually. Future plans include in-room devices with digital image projection availability. This will lead to more changes for the physicians and requires a plan to make the transition a smooth one.

References

1 Brailer D. Recasting IT strategy. *Hospitals and Health Networks Magazine*. October 2004 [extracted from an editorial].

2 Grodin S. *Purple Cow: Transform Your Business by Being Remarkable*. Portfolio Publishing; 2003.

SECTION II

CORE EHR COMPONENTS

CHAPTER 4

The Assessment Process

Fanny Hawkins, EdD, RHIA, CPHQ

The care delivery process begins with the initial assessment. At this point a wide range of EHR resources can be leveraged, including the longitudinal health record, personal health record, and information from other providers. Furthermore, outputs from the assessment such as allergies, problems, and patient history become critical data for downstream EHR functions such as medication management, care planning, and clinical decision support. This chapter describes the main elements of the EHR related to the assessment process and some of the challenges involved in implementation. Chapter 7 provides a broader discussion of clinical documentation.

The EHR captures data and information concerning a patient's health, uniquely representing patients and serving as a dynamic resource for the healthcare industry. When reviewed over time, it paints a longitudinal picture of health problems and services. The goal of the EHR is real-time collection, done once; all downstream users benefit from the process and duplicate or inconsistent data collection is avoided. Healthcare delivery is enhanced when a patient's history and physical exam, problem list, medication list, and other components of assessment information are electronically collected at the beginning of the visit or encounter and then leveraged by other caregivers. The major HL7 EHR standard functions for the assessment process are presented in Table 4-1.

Paper-based patient data often results in healthcare teams working from fragmented and incomplete medical histories. Accurate, accessible, and shareable health information is a well-accepted prerequisite of good healthcare. However, the healthcare system in the United States continues to accept illegible handwriting and other less-than-ideal

---

Jennifer Guite, RN, MS, contributed Case Study 3 on Nursing Assessment "Jump Starts" Care.

documentation practices that diminish the quality of healthcare information through reduced accuracy, accessibility, and shareability. This reduced quality influences five major areas in the healthcare system:[1]

- Patient safety is affected by inadequate information, illegible entries, misinterpretations, and insufficient interoperability.
- Public safety, a major component of public health, is diminished by the inability to collect information in a coordinated, timely manner at the provider level in response to epidemics and the threat of terrorism.
- Continuity of patient care is adversely affected by the lack of shareable information among patient care providers.
- Healthcare economics are adversely affected, with information capture and report generation costs currently estimated to be well over $50 billion annually.
- Clinical research and outcomes analysis are adversely affected by a lack of uniform information capture that is needed to facilitate the derivation of data from routine patient care documentation.

Table 4-1: The HL7 EHR Prescription: Assessments

Key Functions Specified for Clinical Documentation by the HL7 EHR Standard*	
Manage problem list (DC.1.1.3.1)	Create and maintain patient-specific problem lists
Manage medication list (DC.1.1.3.2)	Create and maintain patient-specific medication lists
Manage allergy and adverse reaction list (DC.1.4.3)	Create and maintain patient-specific allergy and adverse reaction lists
Manage patient history (DC.1.1.4)	Capture, review, and manage medical procedural/surgical, social and family history including the capture of pertinent positive and negative histories, patient-reported or externally available patient clinical history
Summarize health record (DC.1.1.5)	Present a chronological, filterable, and comprehensive review of a patient's EHR, which may be summarized, subject to privacy and confidentiality requirements
Support for standard assessments (DC.2.1.1)	Offer prompts to support the adherence to care plans, guidelines, and protocols at the point of information capture

*For a comprehensive and current list of HL7 EHR standard components, visit www.hl7.org/ehr.

CLINICAL VOCABULARIES

Clinical data set, vocabulary, terminology, and classification system: these terms are often used interchangeably.[2] The concept of a universally-accepted, standardized clinical language is fundamental to implementation of the EHR. Healthcare outcomes can be reliable and meaningful with the consistent collection of detailed clinical data. The use of a standardized vocabulary allows information to be analyzed, specific, precise, and comparable.

Data Set

A data set is a list of recommended data elements—such as age, principal diagnosis, or level of functioning—with uniform definitions. Each data element should have a single stated definition and purpose. It should also have a unique name or data dictionary established. A data set should also have some interrelationship between the data elements that are defined. Examples of a data set could include a physician's index as well as something more complex, such as the Uniform Hospital Discharge Data Set.

Clinical Vocabulary

A clinical vocabulary is a list or collection of clinical words or phrases with their meanings. Examples of clinical vocabularies include the Systematized Nomenclature of Medicine (SNOMED) from the College of American Pathologists, the Read Codes from Britain's National Health Service, and the Unified Medical Language System (UMLS) from the National Library of Medicine.

Clinical Terminology

A clinical terminology is a set of words or expressions together with a definition used within a certain field. It is a system of clinical terms of preferred terminology or a nomenclature. Examples include defined terms such as a neuroma or colitis, abbreviations such as SLE for systemic lupus erythematosus, or CMV for cytomegalovirus, as well as synonyms of terms.

Classification System

A classification system is the systematic representation of terms and concepts and the relationships between them. Examples include ICD-9-CM, CPT, ICD-10-PCS, and the North American Nursing Diagnosis Association Taxonomy (NANDA).

Clinical data sets, vocabularies, terminologies, and classification systems allow data to be collected, processed, and retrieved for clinical purposes and also provide data to support administrative, statistical, and reimbursement functions.[3] They are particularly important in the assessment process, where critical documentation begins that will impact care in the remainder of the encounter. However, their implementation in community hospitals and ambulatory practice facilities has been slow.

ASSESSMENTS

How care is documented varies among different patient care settings. In acute care and critical care settings, the focus is on charting assessment findings, nursing interventions, patient responses, and patient outcomes.

Professional organizations such as the American Nurses Association (ANA) and regulatory agencies such as the Joint Commission on Accreditation of Healthcare Organizations (JCAHO) and the Center for Medicare & Medicaid Services (CMS) require that documentation include initial and ongoing assessments, any variations from the assessment, patient teaching, response to therapy, and relevant statements made by the patient. Current JCAHO standards direct all healthcare facilities to establish policies about the frequency and documentation of patient assessment.

Healthcare practitioners spend a large portion of their workdays documenting clinical data and the care that was delivered. Frequently, documentation is completed hours after the fact, requiring practitioners to rely on their memories or scribbled notes for accuracy. Using the EHR to conduct patient assessments enables practitioners to focus more on the important patient care tasks at hand and less on documentation. Access to electronic documentation at the bedside also streamlines the care process and assists all clinicians in making better patient care decisions. Communication between caregivers is enhanced since patient data is now available in real-time to any caregiver with access to the system.

One of the key benefits of electronic documentation of assessments is the ability to default forward to the next assessment the information from the previous one. Instead of completely re-documenting the assessment, the caregiver can update the assessment with only those changes to the patient's condition. This is particularly useful with assessments that are repeated at the beginning or ending of each shift or at some other frequent interval. Discussion of the issues with defaulting documentation occurs in Chapter 7. Selected studies relating to the benefits of automating assessments are presented in Table 4-2.

Table 4-2: The Evidence-Based EHR: Assessments

Selected Studies Supporting the Benefits of Electronic Assessments	
Benefits of patient assessments using the EHR[4]	• Improve legibility • Decrease recording time and cost • Improve communication among healthcare team members • Provide greater access to medical data for patient care, education, research, and quality improvement
Quality of documentation improved in the ED[5]	Electronic charting in an emergency department improved assessment documentation as well as downstream processes including testing, treatment and discharge instructions
Computerized documentation produces numerous benefits[6]	Study of computerized clinical documentation in a pediatric ICU found: • Improved legibility and completeness of documentation • Data with better accessibility and accuracy • No change in time spent in direct patient care or charting by nursing staff • Improved JCAHO documentation compliance • A decrease in time and resource use for audits • Improved reimbursement because of the ability to reconstruct lost charts • Elimination of cost of printing forms

Patient assessments are the foundation of patient care. Yet in a paper-based environment, the documentation of those assessments is often incomplete, inconsistent, and not done in a timely manner. When caregivers capture patient assessment data using a clinical documentation system, the entire process is more efficient. Standard assessment and charting screens that have been designed to adhere to care standards and regulatory requirements help ensure the quality and completeness of documentation. When documenting care electronically, a nurse can review admission history data from a previous visit, and, if still applicable, pull it forward for the current visit, revising only those items that have changed. The organization can flag specific data fields on the assessment screens as "required" so that the nurse must complete assessment responses for critical documentation items such as functional and nutritional status. As an added patient safety benefit, required fields also prompt the novice nurse to remember to perform necessary tasks. An implementation checklist for assessments is provided in Table 4-3.

Problem List

A problem list is used to document and track a patient's problems. It provides the clinician with a current and historical view of the patient's healthcare problems across clinical specialties and allows each identified problem to be traceable through the system in terms of treatment, test results, and outcome.

Table 4-3: Implementation Checklist for Assessments

☑ Consolidate assessments when automating to ensure data from one assessment on a patient can be reused on another assessment provided.
☑ Enable use of the longitudinal record and provide flowsheets and data views that highlight important information from the patient's history.
☑ Take advantage of mobile devices if applicable to improve the assessment's timeliness and accuracy.
☑ Envision how information collected in the assessment may be used downstream for clinical decision support.
☑ Carefully audit assessment compliance, particularly the collection of allergy information.

Successful implementation of the problem list is most often found in the ambulatory care setting, where it is an essential element of the EHR. It also is designed to be used by medical and coding clerks. The use of the problem list in the acute care setting is more challenging and is achieved frequently using a free text field completed at time of admission. The value of the problem list in acute care settings can be significant when it is joined with clinical decision support rules to better direct and guide care. However, few acute care organizations have successfully implemented the type of codified problem list required to enable clinical decision support.

Medication and Allergy List

To facilitate the ongoing provision of effective medical care, a patient's allergies/sensitivities to medications, foods, and biological preparations should be accurately recorded and prominently displayed in the EHR. Having a single reliable source of information and a standard process for identifying allergies is critical. If a patient has no known allergies or history of adverse reactions, this should be prominently noted. Allergies to environmental allergens, food, pets, and so forth should also be noted, as they can affect patient behavior.

The medication list includes every medication ordered or prescribed for a patient. In the acute care setting, it should include medications the patient was using prior to admission. Medication errors, such as prescribing contraindicated medicines or prescribing the wrong medicine dose, are the number one source of error in family practices in the U.S. A number of these errors could be prevented if patients' medication records were more accurate, up-to-date, and accessible. However, maintaining such records is a challenge. Patients change their medications frequently, often visit more than one physician, and use undocumented over-the-counter medications.[7]

USING EXTERNAL INFORMATION IN THE ASSESSMENT PROCESS

Continuity of Care Record (CCR)

The CCR will create a major transformation of the intake and assessment process for most providers over the next five years. Today, when a patient visits a physician's office or a hospital, a significant amount of time is spent collecting information through the assessment process. However, much of this information is likely to have already been acquired by a referring or other provider. This redundant information collection is labor intensive, frustrating for the patient, and error prone.

The CCR allows a provider to electronically communicate information about a patient to another provider. It is supported by a wide variety of groups including the American Academy of Family Physicians, which has been integrally involved in determining the CCR's clinical content. The content described is strictly limited to those elements considered most relevant during the hand-off of a patient's care. ASTM International, and more recently HL7, are responsible for developing the technical specifications. The CCR is an XML-based standard intended to promote interoperability as well as portability. The standard was approved in 2004 but final specifications are not expected until later in 2005.

The expectation for the CCR is that it will become a standard feature of any vendor-supplied EHR system. CCR data would be collected through the normal course of clinical documentation by the acute care or ambulatory provider and entered into the provider's EHR (Table 4-4). When a provider refers, transfers, or discharges a patient, his or her CCR would be sent to the receiving provider. The XML format of the CCR allows for flexibility in the data exchange. Depending on the capabilities of the exchanging partners, the exchange could be a direct transaction, a Web document, a file attached to an e-mail, or even a document printed and delivered in hardcopy.

For example, the CCR could be used by an ambulatory practice to refer a patient to a specialist or to an acute care facility. An acute care facility could use the CCR to update the patient's primary care physician or provide information to a long-term care provider about the patient's encounter. For the receiving provider, the CCR could become a valuable tool in the assessment process by reducing the amount of information that needs to be collected directly from the patient and providing the opportunity to electronically populate the provider's EHR without user intervention.

Table 4-4: CCR Data Categories

1. CCR identifying information	Info re "from/to" providers/clinicians Dates Purpose
2. Patient identifying information	
3. Patient insurance/financial	
4. Advance directives	
5. Patient's health status	Family history Adverse reactions/allergies/etc. Social history & health risk factors Medications Immunizations Vital signs/physiological measurements Laboratory results/observations Procedures/imaging
6. Care documentation	
7. Care plan recommendation	
8. Practitioners	

While the CCR has great promise, there will still be some bumps in the road to its implementation. Because standards do not exist for all of the information transferred in the CCR, there is a significant amount of "textual" data that will not be able to be automatically loaded into a receiving EHR system. The CCR's focus has been on a core set of data; it is not clear what "extensions" will be developed or when. Finally, how the CCR will be implemented with Regional Health Information Organizations (RHIOs) is yet to be determined. Nonetheless, the CCR is expected to be adopted quickly by provider organizations once the standard is set and vendors release the capability in their products.

Personal Health Record (PHR)

The Personal Health Record, like the CCR, is a capability of the EHR that has the potential to enhance the assessment process. (Other emerging trends surrounding the assessment process are listed in Table 4-5.) The PHR enables the patient to maintain his/her own health record, brings timely information to established and new caregivers, encourages patient involvement in discussions and decisions, and helps to document and monitor healthcare factors such as medications, immunizations, allergies, diagnostic tests, and questions and answers. The Markle Foundation defines the PHR as "a single, *person-centered* [emphasis in original] system designed to track and support health activities across one's entire life experience, not limited to a single organization or a single health care provider."[8]

Table 4-5: Three-Year Prognosis: Assessments

☑ Clinical vocabulary standards including SNOMED will be more widely featured in vendor products and utilized by providers.
☑ The CCR will become a standard feature of all EHRs and providers will quickly adopt it as a routine part of the assessment process.
☑ Personal health records will be widely used by patients with chronic diseases.
☑ Assessment data will frequently be precollected online from patients via patient portals prior to an admission or visit.

Like the CCR, the PHR is a capability of the EHR that has the potential to enhance the assessment process. The PHR enables the patient to maintain his/her own health record spanning visits and providers. A patient's assessment can be enhanced when he or she brings PHR information to an established, or new, caregiver. The PHR presents a more complete picture of the patient's condition to the provider and encourages patient involvement in discussions and decisions made during the visit.

The Markle Foundation, which sponsored the Connecting for Health initiative, conducted a national survey to assess public interest in the PHR. It found that more than 70% of respondents would use a PHR and that the greatest interest was from the chronically ill, frequent users of healthcare, and people caring for elderly parents.[9] A survey conducted by Agarwal found that the primary reasons respondents used the PHR were to record family medical history (26%) and to track physician visits (21%), medications (19%), and lab results (14%). The value of the PHR fell into three categories: (a) it helped respondents stay organized, such as by keeping appointments, refilling prescriptions, and complying with healthcare regimens such as staying on schedule to test blood sugar and monitoring weight; (b) it improved respondents' communication with their providers; and (c) it was convenient to have their information in one place for emergency situations.

The PHR is delivered through a variety of mechanisms including USB drives, flash memory cards, and patient portals. PHR products include features for self monitoring, maintenance of clinical records, communication with providers, and decision support.

Some PHR products offer the user the capability to produce a CCR-like communication that could be integrated into a provider's EHR. Providers themselves are sometimes offering PHRs to particular populations of patients who can benefit from self-monitoring, such as patients with diabetes and asthma.

PHRs are part of the Office of the National Coordinator's Framework for Strategic Action (see Chapter 1). This, together with increasing public interest, vendor development, and provider interest, suggests PHR growth over the next few years. Creating enthusiasm for the PHR beyond chronic disease patient populations, and personally maintained PHR information will be shared with and integrated into provider EHRs and RHIO clearinghouses are important challenges that need to be addressed in the future if PHRs are to become a significant locale on the EHR landscape.

Case Study 3: Nursing Assessment "Jump Starts" Care

Organization:	Christiana Care Health System, Wilmington, Delaware
Acute Care Facilities:	2
Staffed Beds:	1,000

Christiana Care's flagship hospital supports over 700 beds and a complex array of ancillary services. Running most days at over 90% capacity, one of the hospital's key objectives is to improve patient throughput. The hospital redesigned its nursing admissions process to "jump start" the delivery of ancillary services to eliminate delays that might impact length of stay.

When patients are admitted to a unit, floor nurses document the online admission assessment in the patient's room using a mobile wireless cart. The assessment, required within the first eight hours after admission, includes a comprehensive medical history, review of systems, documentation of allergies, and identification of special problems. When the online form is electronically signed, a series of appropriate decision support rules automatically fire against the data entered in the form. The criteria defined in these rules determine what referrals should be made and to which ancillary departments they are destined. Referral orders are automatically generated, and in turn place tasks on the online work lists of the ancillary departments, including respiratory, dietary, care management, pastoral care, and others. Each department-specific task list is designed to ensure that the department's defined teams have their own lists. This presorted design facilitates the immediate scheduling of the service without additional clerical support. As a task is completed, the original order that was automatically generated upon admission is updated as "complete," notifying nursing of the service delivered. This instant notification of the need for service and then the completion of service to the appropriate caregivers ultimately foster the collaboration of patient care.

The benefits of the system far outweigh the challenges that were endured during its initial implementation. Only a few significant implementation challenges were encountered. One challenge included finalizing clear and concise criteria to develop the decision support rules. Since each specific criterion needed to meet the requirements of both the nursing and ancillary departments, a substantial amount of project time was needed for multiple teams to collaborate to determine the rules design. A second challenge occurred when trying to ensure full compliance of the admission process. Staff sometimes did not complete the form within the required timeframe and sometimes produced multiple forms for the same patient. Although the adoption by the nursing staff has been exceptionally strong, audit reports are generated daily to identify specific form problems. For example, a list is produced of patients who have no admission form found for the current visit or forms that are incomplete. Follow-up occurs daily with the staff members caring for these patients to provide additional educational opportunities. Compliance is improving dramatically, as staff members become more familiar with the tool and the revised admission process.

References

1   Nayer M, Miller S. Anticipating error: Identifying weak links in the electronic healthcare environment. *Journal of AHIMA*. 2004; 75(8).

2   AHIMA Coding Policy and Strategy Committee. Clarification of Clinical Data Sets, Vocabularies, Terminologies, and Classification. *Journal of AHIMA*. 1999; 70(2).

3   Johns ML. *Health Information Management Technology: An Applied Approach*. Chicago: AHIMA; 2002.

4   *Mastering Documentation, Second Edition*. Springhouse, PA: Springhouse Corp.; 1999; pp 1–16, 17, 42, 61–102.

5   Buller-Close K, et al: Heterogeneous effect of an emergency department expert charting system. *Annals of Emergency Medicine*. 2003; 41(5):644-652.

6   Menke JA, et al. Computerized clinical documentation system in the pediatric intensive care unit. BMC Medical Informatics & Decision Making. 2001; 1(1):3.

7   www.aafp.org/fpm/20030300/refs.

8   www.markle.org; (Markle Foundation, Personal Health Working Group, Final Report, July 1, 2003,

9   www.markle.org.

CHAPTER 5

Provider Order Management

Donald Levick, MD, MBA

Although computerized provider order entry (CPOE) is one of the most important components of the EHR and has the potential for driving significant benefits for patient safety, estimates of CPOE adoption rates by acute care providers were only about 5% at the end of 2004. This chapter highlights the EHR and user-readiness prerequisites for a successful implementation as well as some exemplary approaches for achieving provider adoption.

Order management and computerized order entry encompass the processes and systems that communicate all forms of orders from an origination point to the appropriate destination, including nursing, pharmacy, and other ancillary departments. In a fully evolved CPOE system, the provider enters the orders electronically, the order is transmitted to the ancillary system (pharmacy, lab, radiology, dietary, etc.), and actions are instigated electronically. A fully developed system would also include clinical decision support (CDS); alerts to users of medication conflicts, interactions, and duplicate orders; and evidence-based support for therapeutic options. (See Table 5-1 for HL7 EHR standard requirements.)

WHY COMPUTERIZED PROVIDER ORDER ENTRY?

Convincing local physicians that CPOE is the correct decision is often a great challenge. The evidence supporting CPOE's patient safety benefit is well documented (Table 5-2). However, physicians do not always identify with the national data. "That doesn't happen here," or "I haven't had any problems with my handwriting," are common responses from the medical staff or clinic users. Presenting physicians with evidence and benefits specific to their practice patterns may be helpful, such as providing local examples of

Mary Otto, RN, BSN, MHSA, contributed Case Study 5 on CPOE in Emergency Department Improves Patient Length of Stay.

problems caused by illegible handwriting and the expediency of order handling with CPOE (orders entered electronically reach the ancillary department instantly, clarity of orders; reduction of call-backs from nursing or ancillary departments).

Table 5-1: The HL7 EHR Prescription*

Key Functions Specified for Order Management by the HL7 EHR Standard	
Place patient care orders (DC.1.4.1)	Capture and track orders based on input from specific care providers.
Order diagnostic tests (DC.1.4.2)	Submit diagnostic test orders based on input from specific care providers.
Manage order sets (DC.1.4.3)	Provide order sets based on provider input or system prompt.
Manage referrals (DC.1.4.4)	Enable the origination, documentation and tracking of referrals between care providers or healthcare organizations, including clinical and administrative details of the referral.
Manage results (DC.1.4.5)	Route, manage and present current and historical test results to appropriate clinical personnel for review, with the ability to filter and compare results.
Support for non-medication ordering (DC.2.4.1)	Identify necessary order entry components for non-medication orders that make the order pertinent, relevant and resource-conservative at the time of provider order entry; flag any inappropriate orders based on patient profile.

*For a comprehensive and current list of HL7 EHR standard components, visit www.hl7.org/ehr.

Table 5-2: The Evidence-Based EHR

Selected Studies Supporting the Benefits of CPOE	
Stat tests are more timely with CPOE	Study on medical-surgical intensive care unit at a teaching hospital found: • Mean time to obtain laboratory specimens decreased from 77 to 21 minutes • Mean time from ordering to laboratory result being reported decreased from 148 to 74 minutes • Mean time from ordering to imaging completed decreased from 96 to 29 minutes[1]
Reminders on corollary orders	25% improvement in ordering of corollary medications by physicians for adult inpatients[2]
Decrease in errors in adult medical, surgical, and ICU inpatients	55% decrease in non-intercepted serious medication errors[3]
CPOE with CDS for all adult inpatients	Improvement in 5 prescribing practices including dosing[4]
Decision support rules key to error prevention	Prescribing errors were evaluated at an academic medical center in the Midwest to determine potential of CPOE to intercept: • 64% of errors rated as likely to be prevented by CPOE • 13% unlikely to be prevented • 22% possibly prevented if clinical decision support rules around dosing and renal function are in place[5]

Real-time CDS is where the true patient safety benefits are realized. This includes alerts for medication allergies and interactions and checking for duplicate orders. More complex CDS examples include rules that automatically calculate creatinine clearance (when ordering medications that are cleared by the kidneys), suggestions for medication doses based on weight or body surface area, and reminders of recent labs when associated medications are ordered.

Real-time and remote access to data—that is, the ability of physicians to work without access to the hardcopy chart—opens up enormous opportunities to improve workflow and efficiency and is one of the most significant physician satisfiers. This provides the clinician access to data from any location: a hospital room, an exam room, conference rooms or lounges, office or home. Real-time, remote data access improves the quality and efficiency of care and communication between clinicians (by facilitating sign-outs and hand-offs), and allows multiple clinicians to simultaneously view the record or orders.

REQUIREMENTS FOR ORDER ENTRY

System Requirements

Order management systems have been evolving for more than 20 years and today have a considerable range of functionality to support patient safety and clinician workflow. However, provider order management brings its own set of unique requirements. The order management functionality is usually only one module in the overall clinical information system. Provider workflow can be compromised significantly if the appropriate array of information is not available to the provider online when entering orders. Table 5-3 provides a list of EHR system components and indicates which are valuable to have in place before implementing CPOE.

Table 5-3: EHR Features Needed for CPOE

EHR Feature	Required for CPOE?
Pharmacy interface	YES – Charting medications online is critical to error reduction. The interface eliminates the need for transcribing or reentering medication orders into the system.
Online medication administration record	HIGHLY DESIRED – Allows nursing to chart electronically and facilitates integration of information (medication administration data and relevant clinical data).
Vital signs and I/O	NO – Desired to increase the amount of clinical data online and to integrate into clinical decision support systems.
Lab/radiology results	YES –CDS systems are driven by this clinical data that must be in the system.
PACS	NO – Desired in order to increase the amount of clinical data available online, but is not required for the provider to do order entry.
Online physician progress notes	NO – Desired to limit the dual systems for physicians.
Online nursing assessments	NO – Clinical documentation is not required for a successful order entry system.

Tight integration between the orders and pharmacy information systems is critical. The orders the provider enters should directly drive the pharmacy system, allowing the pharmacy staff to verify the orders online without having to reenter them. In an ideal deployment, this system would also drive dispensing the medications through a robot system and/or dispensing cabinets. Having the pharmacy system integrated with the ordering system also supports online charting of medication administration by nursing. Finally, it is helpful to have an integrated approach to providing decision support so that the ordering provider, pharmacist, and nurse all receive the same decision support alerts and have access to documentation of alerts that have been over-written.

Organizational Requirements

Implementing a CPOE is a tremendous cultural and organizational change. Consequently, support from all levels of the organization is required for success. Champions for the change should come from the rank and file. However, support must exist at all levels, including senior administrators who will need to approve funding and will likely be approached by informal leaders who are resisting, and members of the board of trustees who may interact with the users on a social level.

Physician leadership, as well as administrative leadership, must be present at all levels and needs to include clinically active physician leaders. Department and clinic chairs, who have leverage to influence physician behavior, must be on board and willing to help confront resistant users. The chief medical officer and other C-level physicians must publicly and privately support the process. Informal opinion leaders must also be brought on board because it is often after the group or department meeting, or in the hallways, that a great impact can be made, either positively or negatively. The most important technique to gain the support of the informal leaders is to involve them early in the process. If they can be made to understand the project's benefits, and can act as physician champions (see below), it will greatly increase the chances for success. Projects that rely too heavily on enthusiastic, computer savvy "early adopters" will likely fail.

A physician champion serves a critical role in the success of any project. One of this person's roles is to articulate the needs of the end users to the technical staff, and to understand the strengths and limitations of the software and how that will impact the end users. A checklist of physician champion attributes is provided in Table 5-4.

Table 5-4: Physician Champion Checklist

☑ Designated time to devote to the project (this time must be clearly carved out from the clinical schedule and appropriately compensated).
☑ Strong interpersonal skills and thick skin.
☑ Ability to interact with both the administration and the medical staff.
☑ Basic technical knowledge (the physician champion should not be too technically oriented, to the point where he or she runs the risk of speaking over the heads of the majority of the medical staff).
☑ Clinical credibility with the medical staff (the physician champion needs to be perceived as a true practicing physician).
☑ Does not function as an analyst or one of the technical staff involved in the project.

PHYSICIAN ISSUES

Great software is in the eye of the beholder. From the physician's standpoint, speed of entry and ease of use are the two most important factors. Physicians are under tremendous pressure to be efficient, both in the inpatient and outpatient arenas. Consequently, any new process that slows them down will not be accepted easily. Physician workflow and how data are entered must be carefully analyzed during the design phase of the project. Physician input from the perspective of all potential users (Table 5-5) is critical at this phase. Moreover, it is important to analyze all existing work processes and avoid automating existing bad processes. Implementing a new system presents a great opportunity to analyze and optimize workflow and work processes with the new system. This can potentially increase the magnitude of change and must be considered carefully.

Table 5-5: CPOE Impact by Physician Type

Physician Type	System Use	Training/Support Requirement	Impact on Workflow	Benefits to User
Community physician: no hospital privileges	None: may look up clinical data, but will not enter orders	Minimal: will need to access system for clinical results review	Minimal	Remote access to clinical data without having to call hospital unit
Community physician with hospital privileges	Moderate: dependent upon volume of hospital admissions	Significant: will require full training and may require ongoing support (due to intermittent use)	Significant: will clearly reduce efficiency during rounds (during learning phase)	All benefits of CPOE as discussed. Remote order entry from office/clinic
Hospitalist	Heavy: will be main users of the system	Significant: will need to be very facile with system. May assist in supporting other physicians	Significant: will completely alter practice pattern	Access to data and order entry from anywhere in the hospital. Will take advantage of all benefits of CPOE as discussed
Specialist with significant in-patient volume	Heavy: depending on use of physician extenders	Significant: will need to be very facile with system	Significant: will alter practice pattern	Access to data and order entry from anywhere in the hospital. Will take advantage of all benefits of CPOE as discussed
Residents	Heavy: will be one of the main users of the system	Significant: will need to be very facile with system	Significant: will be learning new workflow as resident and therefore change may be minimal	Access to data and order entry from anywhere in the hospital. Will take advantage of all benefits of CPOE as discussed

The learning curve to become proficient with the software must be as short as possible. Physicians, like most people, will tolerate disruption in their typical process for only so long. They must feel that they are making progress and becoming more proficient over time to maintain the momentum. Ease of use of the system is also important since many physicians will use the system intermittently: physicians may round in the hospital one week out of every month. Thus, they will naturally lose some of the skill they might have developed during their previous rounding sessions. The more intuitive the system, the easier it will be for physicians to retain those skills. The effect of this intermittent exposure is also true in the ambulatory environment.

The system should be able to be tailored to accommodate ongoing requests by users. Ideally, the end users will be able to tailor some features of the system themselves, such as favorite orders and list management. When this is not possible, the support team should be able to turn requests around in a reasonable amount of time. If this does not occur, users will claim that the system and the IT team are inflexible and unresponsive. This type of negative publicity can severely hurt the chances for successful implementation.

Alert functions and clinical decision support are great benefits of automated systems. The granularity of alerts should be able to be tailored or adjusted. Each organization will have to decide who has the authority to change the level of the alert functions. Eliminating alerts completely will negate some of the true value of a CPOE system. However, too many alerts will result in the physicians and users ignoring the information. Finding the appropriate balance is key to successful implementation of clinical decision-support systems. It is also valuable to provide physicians with information on the benefits of clinical decision support through, for example, reporting the number of decision support alerts that were presented to and accepted by physicians. These provide a good indicator of how the system is reducing error and improving care.

TRAINING AND SUPPORT

Training physicians to use the system presents several unique challenges.

Busy physicians are reluctant to give up the time required to learn to use the system. Therefore, organizations may need to compensate the physicians for training time. Training should be at the convenience of the physician and not of the training staff. Often, this results in training occurring during early morning hours, at the end of the day, or even on weekends. Another challenge to be taken into account during training is individual computer literacy. Many physicians are quite comfortable with medical technology but have limited experience with computers. Training of these physicians may need to occur in two phases: first getting them accustomed to the computer, and then teaching them to use the ordering system. In addition, physicians may require periodic retraining, due to intermittent exposure to this system. Such retraining can occur either as a separate session or "on the fly" by support personnel. Again, the physician should drive the demand.

Support is one of the most visible aspects of any implementation. The support team interacts with the users more than anyone else involved in the project. Consequently, creating the right support team and providing appropriate support can make or break the success of the project. Often, the personnel providing support are also involved in training. For the users, this provides continuity and promotes an easy transition process.

Critical characteristics of the support team and support process include:

- Individuals must have excellent interpersonal skills and be able to deal with physician frustration.
- Team members must possess in-depth knowledge of the software and understanding of the physician workflow involved. A separate support team outside of the organization's help desk is needed.
- Initial support must be 24/7, with on-site coverage for the first several weeks of a go-live. Ideally, the number of support personnel will approximate the number of users at any given time, resulting in one-to-one education and support.
- Post-live support must remain easily accessible and responsive. It is a challenge to encourage physicians to call the support team; it is devastating if the response is delayed or if the help desk person is not knowledgeable about the problem.
- A different venue should be considered for non-urgent questions and suggestions by the physicians. This could include e-mail, Web-based forms, or a separate phone line.

- It is important to remember that support does not stop after go-live. New physicians and users are always coming online, enhancements and other changes need to be communicated to the users, and physicians who do not use the system on a daily basis will require ongoing support.

ORDER SETS

Order sets are groups of orders that facilitate the order entry process. They represent a great value-added feature that can be used to build physician acceptance of the system. However, there are numerous issues that must be addressed when implementing them.

The level of specificity of the order set must be decided early in the process. At the department or group level, order sets present a great opportunity to standardize care and provide order guidelines that are evidence-based. However, physicians may request that order sets be created at group- or physician-specific levels that differ from the standard order set. Producing such specific order sets may lead to increased acceptance of the CPOE system but will result in variability of care. The decision whether or not to allow personalized order sets needs to be made early in the process and communicated clearly to physicians so their expectations can be managed appropriately.

The approval process for computerized order sets must also be determined beforehand. In the paper world, the paper order set passes through various committees (such as committees for forms, nursing care, and therapeutics), resulting in long delays between the creation of the order set and its implementation. Leadership needs to decide whether computerized order sets are required to go through the same approval process or a streamlined version.

Rapid turnaround of computerized order sets can provide another value-added feature that enhances acceptance of the system. Hospitals often have hundreds of paper order sets on the units. Many of these are out of date or are never used. Determining which order sets should be converted to computerized order sets first will impact both resource allocation on the technical side and physician acceptance on the user side. The "low hanging fruit" should be selected first: order sets that are current, easy to convert, and are actually used by the physicians represent appropriate targets. These order sets can be used to demonstrate the benefits of the system and efficiencies of electronic order entry and can stimulate ideas for future order sets by the physicians.

TURNING OVER THE ROCKS

Planning and implementing a CPOE system impacts virtually every user and ancillary system (Table 5-6). Work processes must be carefully evaluated during the planning stages and adapted to the changes inherent in CPOE system. The potential exists to automate inefficient and potentially dangerous existing manual work processes, resulting in loss of potential efficiency gains. Several examples are described below.

The timing for medication administration is a clear example of orders that live in the "gray area." In the paper world, physicians often order medications without specifying the exact administration times, leaving the nurse or pharmacist to interpret the intent. This practice can result in extra doses or missed doses. In a CPOE system, administration times are required, forcing the physician to determine when the first dose should be administered.

Table 5-6: CPOE Impact by Staff Type

Staff	Change of Role/Impact	Comments
Unit clerk	• Will no longer enter most orders • Continues to coordinate care on unit	• May need to enter phone orders or orders from non-users • Studies have shown no true reduction in workforce with CPOE
Nurses	• Will need to look online for orders • Will chart medications online • Will be more efficient after facile with system	• CPOE eliminates nurses' 'translator' role – interpreting physician orders or meaning • Face-to-face communication with physicians may decrease
Pharmacy staff	• No longer enter/verify handwritten orders • Will look online to verify medication orders • Decreased time interpreting physician orders • Potential increase time in clinical 'rounding'	• Role will change from interpreting handwritten orders to cleaning up electronic orders (e.g., correcting start times)
Ancillary staff	• May need to look online to find new orders • Orders will be entered in 'physician-ese' and not in ancillary terms	• Opportunity to standardize ancillary orders

Consultations represent another common area of miscommunication. When physicians handwrite consultation orders, they often will not supply the acuity of the consultation (i.e., urgent versus non-urgent) or an appropriate reason for the consultation. Without proper planning, the CPOE system can easily duplicate these deficiencies.

The process for transportation of patients for diagnostic studies must be evaluated. The diagnostic suite will often request the mode of transport for the patient to be part of the diagnostic study order (i.e., wheelchair, stretcher, ambulatory). Physicians may not know the mode of transport nor will they feel that providing this information as part of the electronic order is their responsibility.

Breakdowns in verbal communication may occur as the CPOE system gains acceptance. Physicians may feel that once they have entered the order into the system, there is no need to communicate with the nurse or other members of the healthcare team. This is especially problematic with STAT orders. Early in the process, the expectation must be set that STAT orders entered electronically still require verbal communication to the appropriate party.

GETTING TO CRITICAL MASS: ACCEPTANCE OF ORDER ENTRY

Despite all the benefits, physicians may still resist a change as significant as CPOE. Other forms of encouragement may need to be investigated. Reward and recognition, an often-used technique in business, is not always as effective with physicians. During the early stages of implementation, when CPOE is not the norm, physician users may be reluctant to be recognized as they have strayed from the norm of the majority of the physician community. Tangible incentives may need to be employed to overcome this reluctance. Examples that have been used in various institutions include contests with prizes for the highest utilizing physicians, awarding of CME credit, or even direct compensation (see Case Study 4 below). One institution, upon reaching 70% physician utilization, declared CPOE as the standard of care and referred any handwritten orders to its patient safety committee for review and follow-up with the physician. Nonetheless, with all its challenges the outlook for CPOE remains strong (Table 5-7).

Table 5-7: Three-Year Prognosis

☑ Improved clinical decision support capabilities will bring evidence-based medicine closer to the point of care.
☑ Continued development of the user interface will improve workflow including voice recognition.
☑ Physicians and other users will have more options to customize the system to support their own individual workflow.
☑ Continued hardware developments will support ease of use and portability.
☑ Payor, regulator, and public pressure to implement CPOE will continue, with CPOE eventually becoming the standard of care.

Case Study 4: Stipends Improve Physician Utilization

Organization:	Lehigh Valley Hospital, Eastern Pennsylvania
Acute Care Facilities:	3
Staffed Beds:	750
Type:	Community Hospital with Residency Program

Lehigh Valley Hospital (LVH) is a 750-bed, three-site system located one hour north of Philadelphia. LVH is an academic community hospital, with several residency programs and 1,100 physicians on active staff (including 200 employed physicians). The majority of the physicians on the medical staff are community-based and independently employed. Attending physicians generate over 60% of the orders on the inpatient units. Consequently, implementing CPOE in this environment presented a tremendous challenge. Early in the process, LVH decided to make CPOE use voluntary for the attending physicians. The hospital implemented CPOE incrementally, with new units being brought live every few months and physicians being brought live by division. After nine months live with several units up, system use by the attending physicians was approximately 35%.

Several techniques were attempted to increase utilization. Public recognition of top users was not well received. Although several physicians supported the project privately, they were reluctant to do so publicly. As the majority of the physicians are community-based and not employed by the hospital, it was difficult for the physician and administrative leadership to apply direct pressure. The main concern of the physician users related to the time involved in learning to use and become facile with the system. Project leadership initiated the "Recognition of Effort" program to compensate the physicians for the learning curve. Over a four-month period, for each month that the physician user met a specified utilization threshold, he or she would receive a stipend to compensate for the extra time taken using the system. The result was that the utilization threshold increased every month of the program. At the end of the four-month program, overall utilization increased to more than 60%. After the program ended, attending utilization began to drift downward. A second program was begun in which each month all users with utilization greater than 60% would be entered into a drawing. The winner of the drawing would receive a voucher for use toward a CME activity. Utilization increased to more than 60% and has remained there since (Figure 5-1).

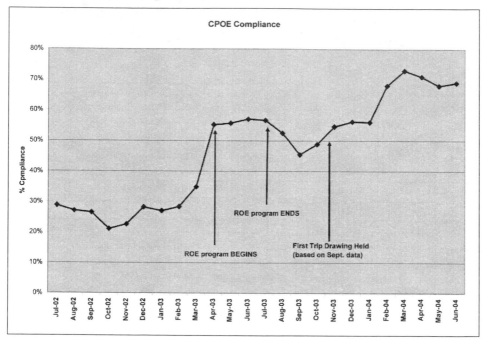

Figure 5-1: CPOE Compliance at Lehigh Valley Hospital

Conclusion: it is clear that even when a strong case is made for CPOE's benefits of patient safety and quality of care, physicians may require more tangible incentives to change their behavior. In an era of decreasing reimbursements, increasing potential for malpractice charges, and increasing regulatory requirements, efficiency has become a critical issue to all physicians. Physicians are quite sensitive to processes that impact on their efficiency but are responsive when that impact is recognized and compensated for.

Case Study 5: CPOE in Emergency Department Improves Patient Length of Stay

Organization: North Broward Hospital District, South Florida
Acute Care Facilities with EDs: 4

The emergency department (ED) is one of the major points of entry for patients at the North Broward Hospital District (NBHD) in South Florida. With four EDs, including two trauma centers, NBHD handles 211,000 visits annually. A key to enhancing patient care and satisfaction in this busy environment was thought to lie in improving the ED patient's turnaround time. After assessing delay factors in the ED patient flow, order entry was identified as a significant contributor. The organization decided to implement CPOE in the emergency department.

From the project's start there were strong clinical and administrative champions readily available. Champions included ED physicians, nurse managers, and an administrator who together comprised the project's steering committee and were actively involved in the project's development. These champions had working knowledge of the ED flow, clinical practice, and department policies and procedures. In addition, the initiative had the support of the physician practice under contract to staff the four EDs, as many of these physicians used CPOE elsewhere.

In developing this initiative, the organization considered what information the physician would need to place an order. Data entry screens were demonstrated at existing physician staff meetings so workflow issues could be addressed in advance. Physicians also determined order set content and were involved in device selection. The bottom line was that the ED physicians were engaged in the design process and were partners in the overall project.

Physician training was provided one-on-one during a two-week window preceding the ED's go-live date. Training was scheduled at the physician's convenience and took one to two hours depending on the physician's prior computer experience. Physicians received on-site support around the clock for the first two weeks of the go-live. Support was provided by trainers familiar with the physicians and training they received. Physicians also assisted one another. Proficiency came quickly as ED physicians are constantly entering orders, looking up results, and navigating the new system.

ED physicians exhibited minimal resistance to change; in those cases where resistance was encountered, a project champion often spent time with the resistant physicians to assist them in using the system.

Today, the ED physician can easily identify online which patients need to be seen, their acuity, chief complaint, and length of time in the ED. The physician has online access to historical patient data (lab results, radiology results, operative reports, etc.), as well as the online triage and nursing assessment documentation that was done upon admission to the ED. During the exam the physician can focus on confirming information already obtained instead of re-collecting it. The physician then directly enters the appropriate orders, often using order sets (abdominal pain, pneumonia, pediatric fever, etc.) that support care practice standardization. Online tracking lists automatically show when results are available. Now, physicians are better equipped to manage the patient's care and length of stay in the ED.

The benefits realized with NBHD's CPOE experience are significant:

- Increase in patient satisfaction scores for waiting time from 70 (out of 100) to 81.
- Reduction in average patient turnaround time from 240 minutes to 193 minutes.
- Reduction in time to enter orders and retrieve results by 21 and 22 minutes, respectively.
- Improved compliance with care standards: For example, compliance with chest pain orders increased from 67% to 99%.

Conclusion: CPOE can be implemented successfully in a small but clinically significant care environment. Organizations pursuing CPOE may want to first explore a controlled implementation to learn the design, training, and support needs for their physician population.

References

1   Thompson W, Dodek PM, Norena M, Dodek J. Computerized physician order entry of diagnostic tests in an intensive care unit is associated with improved timeliness of service. *Critical Care Medicine*. 2004; 32(6):1306.

2   Overhage JM, Tierney WM, Xiao-Hua Z, McDonald CJ. A randomized trial of "corollary orders" to prevent errors of omission. *Journal of American Medical Informatics Association*. 1997; 4(5):364–375.

3   Bates DW, Leape LL, Cullen DJ, et al. Effect of computerized physician order entry and a team intervention on prevention of serious medication errors. *JAMA*. 1998; 280:1311–1316.

4   Teich JM, Merchia PR, Schmiz JC, et al: Effects of computerized physician order entry on prescribing practices. *Arch Intern Med*. 2000; 160:2741–2747.

5   Bobb A, Gleason K, Husch M, et al: The epidemiology of prescribing errors: The potential impact of computerized prescriber order entry. *Arch Intern Med*. 2004; 164:785–792.

Bibliography

The Advisory Board. *Computerizied Physician Order Entry—Securing Physician Acceptance*. Washington, DC; 2004.

Ash JS, Stavri PZ, Kuperman GJ: A consensus statement on considerations for a successful CPOE implementation. *Journal American Medical Informatics Association*. 2003; 10(3):229–234.

Bates DW, Teich JM, Lee J, et al. The impact of computerized physician order entry on medication error prevention. *Journal American Medical Informatics Association*. 1999; 6(4):313–321.

Kuperman GJ, Gibson RF. Computer physician order entry: Benefits, costs and issues. *Annals of Internal Medicine*. 2003; 139(1):31.

Kuperman GJ, Teich JM, Gandhi JK, Bates DW: Patient safety and computerized medication ordering at Brigham and Women's Hospital. *Joint Commission Journal on Quality Improvement*. 2001; 27(10):509–521.

Lee F, Teich JM, Spurr CD, Bates DW. Implementation of physician order entry: User satisfaction and self-reported usage patterns. *Journal American Medical Informatics Association*. 1996; (3)1:42–55.

Levick D, Lukens HF, Stillman PL. You've led the horse to water; now how do you get him to drink: Managing change and increasing utilization of computerized provider order entry. *Journal of Healthcare Information Management*. 2005; (19)1:70–75.

Levick D, O'Brien D. CPOE is much more than computers. *Physician Executive*. November 2003; 48.

Mekhjian HS, Kumar RR, Kuehn L, et al. Immediate benefits realized following implementation of physician order entry at an academic medical center. *Journal American Medical Informatics Association*. 2002; 9(5):529–539.

Sengstack PP, Gugerty B: CPOE systems: Success factors and implementation issues. *Journal of Healthcare Information Management*. 2004; (18)1:36–45.

CHAPTER 6

The Medication Process

Toby Clark, RPh, MSc, FASHP

The medication process is one of the most complex and clinically critical components of the EHR. It involves multiple systems and interfaces as well as a wide array of stakeholders, including physicians, nursing, and other ancillary departments in addition to pharmacy. Moreover, no other single process within healthcare has a greater impact on patient safety and outcomes. However, for years the pharmacy system has been a "black box" in many organizations. The push toward CPOE and point-of-care medication administration presents a challenge to the continuity of the medication process and the systems that support it across the range of disciplines. This chapter examines the various components of this process and their relation to the EHR.

STEPS IN THE MEDICATION SYSTEM

Today's acute care medication system is a complex mixture of the functions and roles of many caregivers as well as administrative and information technology professionals. The medication system has five major components:

- Prescribing;
- Pharmacy therapy monitoring/order interpreting/verifying;
- Dispensing;
- Nursing order interpretation/administration; and
- Multidisciplinary medication therapy monitoring.

Stanley S. Kent, RPh, MS, and Lynn Boecler, PharmD, MS, contributed Case Study 6 on EMAR Synchronizes Nursing and Pharmacy. Donnie La Rue contributed Case Study 7 on Bar Coding Reduces Medication Errors.

While physicians order most prescriptions, nurses, pharmacists, and other therapists also participate in the process. Pharmacy has several steps in the process. These include proactive therapy monitoring and order interpretation, checking and verification, and medication preparation and dispensing. The clinical pharmacy functions of proactive therapy monitoring include the direct, specific, patient care activities of
- Collecting patient-specific information;
- Determining the presence of medication-therapy problems;
- Summarizing patient's healthcare needs;
- Specifying pharmacotherapeutic goals;
- Designing a pharmacotherapeutic regimen;
- Designing a monitoring plan;
- Designing a regimen and corresponding monitoring plan with the patient and other health professionals;
- Initiating the regimen;
- Monitoring the effects of the regimen; and
- Redesigning the regimen and monitoring plan.

The use of computer systems greatly enhances the order interpretation, checking, and verification process. Nonetheless, the need for pharmacist review is vital because not all elements of the prescription predispensing processes are or can be computerized.

Nursing has the vital responsibilities of second or dual medication order interpretation and the administration and/or discontinuance of the intended medication. All caregivers participate in the important process of medication therapy monitoring to help ensure that the correct selection of the medication and dosage form is administered to the patient in a safe and therapeutic regimen for the intended therapeutic response.

It should be remembered that the medication system exists in all locations of the institution, including patient care units, emergency room, special procedures areas (e.g., GI lab, cath lab), operating and recovery rooms, radiology, outpatient clinics, or any other areas where medications are ordered and administered. The major HL7 EHR standard functions for the medication process are presented in Table 6-1.

Table 6-1: The HL7 EHR Prescription

Key Functions Specified for Medication Management by the HL7 EHR Standard*	
Order medication (DC.1.3.1)	Create prescriptions or other medication orders with detail adequate for correct filling and administration. Provide information regarding compliance of medication orders with formularies.
Manage medication administration (DC.1.3.2)	Present to appropriate clinicians the list of medications that are to be administered to a patient, under what circumstances, and capture administration details.
Pharmacy communication (DC.3.2.2)	Provide features to enable secure bidirectional communication of information electronically between practitioners and pharmacies or between practitioner and intended recipient of pharmacy orders.

* For a comprehensive and current list of HL7 EHR standard components, visit www.hl7.org/ehr.

PROFESSIONAL PRACTICE STANDARDS

Medication system professional practice standards have been promulgated by the American Society of Health-System Pharmacists (ASHP). The ASHP guidance documents (statements and guidelines) have been written to cover the areas of automation and information technology, drug distribution and control, education and training, ethics, formulary management (medication use policy), government and regulation, medication misadventures, medication therapy, pharmaceutical industry, and pharmacy management. Nursing standards of practice have been elaborated in detail by the American Nurses Association (ANA) and are also very helpful in the design of the medication system.

In 2003 the Institute for Safe Medication Practices issued a document entitled "Draft Guideline for Safe Electronic Communication of Medication Orders" in an effort to assist in reducing errors associated with computerized medication processes. These guidelines are useful in both CPOE components as well as the pharmacy and nursing portions of the electronic health record system. To truly make the EHR safe and avoid problems, healthcare technology systems need to use a set of accepted standards for the electronic communication of medication information.

MEDICATION SYSTEM TECHNOLOGY MODEL (MSTM)

The Medication System Technology Model is a tool to explain in detail the various elements of the EHR and the technology communication facets of the medication system (Figure 6-1). The MSTM tool aids in understanding the complex medication system by caregivers, administrators, technology specialists, vendor partners, and payors to serve patients with the highest levels of safety, quality and productivity.

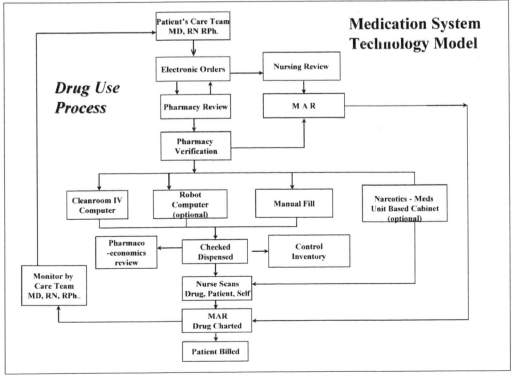

Figure 6-1: Medication System Technology Model

The medication system technology strategy is a functional description by diagram of the flow of electronic communication within the medication system for one hospital. It was originally designed as part of an EHR initiative at the University of Illinois at Chicago Medical Center. The MSTM is valuable in explaining the future-state medication system to key stakeholders such as medical center administrators, medical staff, nursing, information technology staff, pharmacy staff, hospital finance department, quality improvement department, and vendors. It was particularly useful during the design, implementation, and operational phases of the EHR. It does not completely depict the various computer systems or their communication mode (one-way/two-way interface/integrated) that are required to accomplish the future-state vision, but rather allows the organization to see the intended outcome with the flow of medication-related information, all with the purpose of increasing safety, quality, and productivity.

CAREGIVER COLLABORATION

Physicians, nurses, and pharmacists have planned, organized, approved, and operated medication systems for a long time. Generally this has been done via the pharmacy and therapeutics committee and/or a nursing-pharmacy committee in the hospital. The importance of caregiver collaboration in concert with information technology cannot be stated too strongly. EHR implementations must be planned with caregivers to assure incorporation of patient safety mechanisms such as those elaborated, for example, by the Institute for Safe Medication Practices, the US Pharmacopeia, and the American Society of Health-System Pharmacists.

Physicians, nurses, pharmacists, and other caregivers must be willing to give the time and energy to support the planning, building, testing, training, and implementation of the electronic tools they will use to care for patients. Obtaining this time commitment is no easy task but is absolutely necessary for an effective EHR to best serve patients. Caregiver collaboration with one another and with information technology is a vital first ingredient in the success of an effective EHR implementation.

THE ORDERS DOCUMENTATION SYSTEM
AND THE PHARMACY SYSTEM

One of the most important system interrelationships in the EHR is how the orders/ documentation system and the pharmacy system are integrated or interfaced. It is strongly desired to have the orders system linked to the pharmacy computer with at least a bidirectional interface and an electronic link to nursing. Some so-called EHR systems only print medication orders in the pharmacy, which in turn must be reentered in the pharmacy system. This causes redundancy, the potential for much greater entry error, and a lack of electronic communication between the prescriber and the verifying pharmacist and potentially the nurse who needs to administer the medication. The orders system can be connected to the pharmacy computer via various mechanisms. These include the one-way interface, bidirectional interface, and an integrated arrangement.

In the undesirable one-way interface situation, orders are electronically transmitted to pharmacy for verification and subsequent processing with no opportunity for nursing to be notified that a pending order has been approved. With the bidirectional interface and the integrated system, medication orders can be sent to pharmacy for verification and nursing can be notified electronically that the order has been placed and verified. The truly integrated system allows for the sharing of common tables between the orders and pharmacy verification software. The opportunity for system errors is greatly increased with multiple drug tables. The sharing of common decision support rules is also important to ensure that prescribers (physicians, dispensers/pharmacists, and documenters/nurses, respiratory therapists, etc.) are all getting the same alerts and have access to any reasons for overrides made by upstream users.

QUALITY OF IMPLEMENTATION CRITICAL TO REALIZING SAFETY BENEFITS

While technology support of the medication process has great benefits (Table 6-2), it also contributes its own set of risks. The United States Pharmacopeia, a Rockville, Maryland-based independent drug-standards agency, reported that nearly 43,000 or 20% of the 235,159 medication error reports it received from 570 hospitals and health systems in 2003 involved computerization or automation. This was the fourth leading cause of errors.

Nearly three-quarters of these errors occur after an order is written but before the medication is administered to the patient. These errors were mostly related to the process of having a nurse or pharmacist transcribe a written order or where drug storage and dispensing devices were used in patient care areas. Distractions were the leading cause of errors, accounting for 56.5% of all computer-related errors.

Table 6-2: The Evidence-Based EHR: Selected Studies Supporting the Benefits of Medication System Automation

ADEs decreased with the adoption of bar code system	Baseline study data was established in a 760-bed hospital where all pediatric and adult patient care areas of the facility were converted to bar coded medication administration (BCMA). The results included a 36% reduction of ADEs, and a 25% reduction in the use of the override function of the unit based cabinets. In addition, billing accuracy was increased.[1]
Institutional benefits of bar code technology	A 243-bed regional hospital took a number of steps to improve safety in its paper system before converting to BCMA. Results included an increase in prevented errors as compared with occurrence reports, with the virtual elimination of omitted or missed doses. Wrong patient errors with intravenous solutions and wrong dose errors are examples of the reduced errors. In addition, a more complete record of medication administration was established.[2]
Bar coding brings to light previously unreported medication errors	A before and after study of the implementation of a BCMA system revealed an increased rate of errors of 18%. The results probably do not show an increase in errors but rather an increase in reporting. Evaluators must have good baseline data before implementation if comparisons are going to be made.[3]
Patient safety and nursing satisfaction increases with bar coding	A Midwestern community hospital realized a 59-70% decrease in medication administration errors on individual nursing units. The study demonstrates how BCMA systems track, reduce, and prevent bedside medication errors while having a positive effect on nursing satisfaction.[4]

Errors from facilities using CPOE were significant, though 99% of these errors did not cause harm to the patient. The most common errors (48.5%) were related to dosing (extra dose, wrong dose, and omission). Errors related to knowledge of the system were the most frequently reported additional cause of error.

These findings suggest that while the promise of technology is great, the quality of its implementation and ongoing support has a major impact on its ability to improve patient safety. The study points out that inadequate training, a confusing user interface, insufficient decision support rules, and user resistance are among the factors that can undermine the goal of improving patient care. All of these, with the exception of the user interface, can be addressed by an organization's implementation. Implementation considerations for the medication process are provided in Table 6-3.

Table 6-3: Implementation Considerations for the Medication Process

Detailed planning	All too frequently, planning for the automated medication system is not sufficiently detailed. • Clearly establish the goals for the medication system and measure them. • Document the process and workflows. • Acquire input from all shifts of pharmacists, nurses and other caregivers; involve EHR champion physicians AND the pharmacy and therapeutics committee members.
Collaborate and build trust	• Continuously build the trust of the design, implementation, and operations personnel in pharmacy, nursing, and information technology. Focus on the mission of the best care possible for the patient.
Patient safety	• Establish ways to evaluate a safe practice using the FMEA techniques
Train-train-train	• Establish mechanisms and incentives for physicians, nurses, pharmacists, respiratory technicians, and all other clinicians and support staff to be trained. • When you think you have trained the nurses, start over again to assure training. • Test the effectiveness of the training and monitor compliance
Assess all the medication areas	• Don't forget the cath lab, special procedures, nuclear medicine, radiology, clinics, and less visible areas where systems and procedures need to be established as well.
Down time procedures	• Establish the down time procedures and then practice them to see if they work.

MEDICATION ADMINISTRATION

One of the most critical yet difficult to implement components of the medication process is the administration record. Studies indicate that about half of medication errors occur at this stage. The EHR is incomplete without an electronic medication administration record (EMAR) and a nursing clinical documentation system. The nurse performs many more functions related to medications when "passing meds." The EMAR should not only enable the nurse to indicate what medication was administered to which patient in what dose at what time but should also support the often complex process of charting required documentation such as pain assessments.

Today the EMAR is defined as the process of electronically documenting, usually online, the information about medication administration. However, many organizations are supplementing the EMAR with bar-coded medication administration (BCMA). A BCMA is an electronic system that allows for machine-readable scanning at the bedside of the patient's armband, the medication, and the nurse to verify the "five rights" of medication administration and chart to the EMAR.

Medications can have either drug-specific or patient-specific bar codes. Both varieties result in the desired code that supports safe drug administration. All medications must be packaged with the bar code and appropriate policies, procedures, and checks should be in place concerning packaging. Bar coding has the potential to be cost-effective. Bar coding patient armbands, caregiver badges, and hospitals can substantially increase patient safety during medication administration.

It must be noted that the much-publicized FDA requirement that drug manufacturers bar code medications by 2007 may not reduce the need for hospitals to bar code medications. If a product is not sold in unit dose packages, it does not have to be bar-code packaged by the manufacturer. No requirement currently exists for manufacturers to offer more of their products in unit dose bar code packaging and in fact, some are now decreasing the number of products in unit dose packages. This will require pharmacies to package more medications themselves.

Implementation of EMAR and BCMA is quite complex. A fully functional implementation involves a significant technology investment (wireless infrastructure, application software, interfaces, bar code scanners, etc.), a fundamental redesign of nursing processes and use of technology, and a major change to pharmacy's process of dispensing, as all or most medications will be required to be bar-coded. Table 6-4 provides some implementation considerations specific to BCMA.

Table 6-4: Implementation Challenges of Bar Code Administration

☑ Use thermal printers for generation of labels because it works better on refrigerated medication doses and will not wear off.
☑ Test the patient armbands to ensure they will work in the system after a patient wears them for 5 days.
☑ Start designing the packaging system early in the process because as much as 75% of the doses need to be bar-code labeled by the pharmacy itself.
☑ Specialty areas such as operating room, recovery room, cath lab, radiology, and respiratory therapy have unique needs and that should be addressed early in the system design.
☑ In the nursing-pharmacy communication process make sure planning has included the afternoon and midnight staff.
☑ Back up plans need to be in place with training and testing to ensure patient safety during down time situations.
☑ Ensure that the bar code scanning equipment is acceptable to the staff nurses who use the devices. Staff nurses should be heavily involved in selecting the devices. Figure out a way for the some of the nurse "champions" to safely "play" with the bar code scanner.
☑ Have plenty of replacement batteries if wireless scanning devices are used.
☑ Pilot the system's low and high medication use areas to assure functioning systems for unit based cabinet meds, other floor stock stocked meds if any, intravenous solutions, and regular schedule and PRN sent from pharmacy in unit dose bins.

Monitoring is a function of determining whether the administered medication is having the desired effect on the patient and to see if any adverse effects are occurring as well. The EHR indeed facilitates this process for the physician, pharmacist, and nurse or other caregiver. This is particularly true when decision support rules have been constructed incorporating the various laboratory functions and other diagnostic tests. Some institutions have used beeper or e-mail notification to send alerts to the caregiver.

E-PRESCRIBING

Any discussion of the medication process and the EHR would not be complete without addressing the quickly emerging area of e-prescribing. (See Table 6-5 for other trends related to the medication process.) Just as the goal of the medication process in the acute care setting is to improve patient care, safety and efficiency, e-prescribing has similar goals but in the ambulatory environment. With more than 3 billion prescriptions dispensed annually mostly on paper, the process of communicating new and refill prescriptions between physician offices and pharmacies is inefficient and costly. In addition, the Center for Information Technology Leadership estimates that 8.8 million adverse drug events occur in the ambulatory setting annually, of which 3 million are preventable.[5] The Institute of Medicine estimates that 1 in 131 ambulatory care deaths annually are due to medication errors. [6]

Table 6-5: Three-Year Prognosis

☑ The EHR will greatly enhance the crossing of inpatient and outpatient boundaries to produce continuity of care. Medication records from multiple sources can come together to decrease costs, increase patient compliance, and decrease the potential for errors on the part of both caregivers and patients.
☑ CDS will be greatly expanded to include intravenous fluid management. Because IV fluids are the most dangerous of high alert medications, much more attention is being focused in this area. One driver to this new focus of medication safety is the use of computerized fluid administration pumps. The computer pumps will be interfaced to the EHR so administration rates and volumes can be monitored as well as the confirmation of the medication being given.
☑ The use of PDAs will increase over the next few years for a host of applications including medication data for formulary management, correct pricing, documentation of observation notes, notification of critical data such as lab values, completion of work lists, and the elimination of paging devices.
☑ The increasing use of automation cabinets in the patient's room means that these units could replace the unit based cabinets for medications and supplies, saving nurses time in the retrieval of products and documentation.
☑ With the use of robots to prepare intravenous admixtures, this automation is currently in production for the batch processing of intravenous piggybacks and reconstitution of vials. With an interface to the EHR, first doses can be prepared more rapidly.

E-prescribing implementations are relatively limited and vary in level of sophistication. Ideally, e-prescribing is a feature of the ambulatory EHR. While the writing of prescriptions is a standard feature of the ambulatory EHR, with e-prescribing the script is not printed but proceeds through two key steps. First, the EHR connects to RxHUB, which provides patient-specific drug benefit information by checking for patient eligibility and formulary compliance of the selected drug. By late 2004, RxHUB contained eligibility data on 150 million individuals, or about 75% of all patients with a pharmacy benefit. Once the physician decides on the prescription, the patient's pharmacy of choice can be selected and the prescription transmitted via SureScripts, a provider of prescription messaging between physician offices and pharmacies. In 2005, SureScripts claimed to have the capability to connect to 85% of the pharmacies in the U.S. and was working with all major EHR vendors to integrate this technology into their ambulatory products.

One major benefit of e-prescribing is to improve the efficiency of the refill process. Over 40% of all prescription transactions are refills. In the mature e-prescribing process for refills the pharmacy receives a request from the patient for a refill. The pharmacy system then recognizes the need for a refill and automatically sends a transaction to the physician office EHR for authorization. When the transaction is received by the physician office EHR it is queued on a worklist for review by the physician. When the refill is approved in the office EHR, a transaction is sent back to the pharmacy authorizing the refill. E-prescribing saves phone calls and faxes that literally consume hours of staff time daily in a large physician practice.

E-prescribing adoption has been slow due to provider costs and concerns about standards. However adoption is expected to increase as EHR vendors increasingly integrate these capabilities into their systems and as standards are developed. The Medicare Prescription Drug Improvement and Modernization Act of 2003 requires that all e-prescriptions paid by the program meet federal e-prescribing standards. The first set of standards was published for public comment in early 2005. These standards are expected to become the de facto standards for all e-prescribing once in place.

Case Study 6: EMAR Synchronizes Nursing and Pharmacy

Organization:	Evanston Northwestern Healthcare, Evanston, Illinois
Acute Care Facilities:	3
Staffed Beds:	720
Type:	Community Hospital with Residency Program

Evanston Northwestern Healthcare (ENH) includes Evanston Hospital (420 beds), Glenbrook Hospital (120 beds), and Highland Park Hospital (180 beds). This acute care teaching-community healthcare system north of Chicago chose to implement a complete electronic health record that included the medication system. ENH, with over 1,600 physicians, 1,000 nurses, 60 pharmacists, and an array of other caregivers and staff sought to improve the overall safety and quality of how medications are ordered, verified, dispensed, clinically monitored and administered. One of the areas of focus for change was the cumbersome and inefficient medication administration record (MAR). The old system was a paper document that was generated by the pharmacy and required manual updates.

Before the establishment of the EHR and the EMAR, physicians wrote paper orders and sent them to the pharmacy for processing. Nursing would generate a new MAR on admission and add new orders in a handwritten fashion. Every 24 hours pharmacy would generate a new MAR from the pharmacy computer system.

With the EHR and the EMAR, the nurse is alerted via an icon on the EMAR screen that an order has been verified by pharmacy and is ready for patient administration at the specified time. In some cases the medication may be sent from pharmacy to the patient care unit or may be removed from the unit based cabinet. After the medication is obtained, it is administered at the appropriate time as scheduled. The nurse charts the given medication on the screen and may be prompted to also chart other data such as pain scale scores for the pain trend charts or blood pressure and pulse for the vitals record. The EMAR system also has a mechanism for the required "double signature" documentation of high alert/high risk medications such as chemos, insulin, PCAs, and controlled substance drips. The system also has a visual queue for overdue meds to alert the nurse to administer the medication in the necessary time frame.

Physicians can generate a written report of meds administered to use "at-a-glance" on rounds. Respiratory therapy and other clinicians also chart medications given on the EMAR.

Benefits include a decrease in doses not being given and a decrease in wrong-time dose administration. Nursing and pharmacy have also experienced a decrease in phone calls because of a screen icon allowing the nurse to request replacement doses. Another benefit was more complete documentation through the use of required fields for certain data at the time of medication charting. The system is also a precursor to the next step in safety enhancement, which is bar code medication administration. Pharmacy and nursing did not attempt to install the bar-coded medication system because it was not available from the vendor and pharmacy needed to install a new pharmacy system as a part of the electronic health record.

Implementation challenges included a review of the EMAR system design and subsequent communication with all of the patient care areas where medication administration documentation occurs. Additionally, in some of the areas no orders are written for medications prior to administration. This includes the operating room where medications such as intra-operative antibiotics are routinely given; these are charted either in the notes section or flowsheet in the EHR. Another challenge was a mechanism for the nurse to change the time of medication administration from the routine schedule. This was resolved with a communication icon that sends a message to pharmacy requesting the change.

Case Study 7: Bar Coding Reduces Medication Errors

Organization:	Peninsula Regional Medical Center, Salisbury, Maryland
Acute Care Facilities:	1
Staffed Beds:	33
Type:	Community Hospital

Peninsula Regional Medical Center is a busy acute care facility with a quest for clinical excellence. Nursing, pharmacy, and others collaborated in the early 2000s to plan and implement a bar code medication administration (BCMA) system. Pharmacy verifies and dispenses and nursing administers over 5,000 doses per day. The BCMA system has been in place and operational since 2002. The operations include a pharmacy computer system with lab test review, dose screening and MAR generation, unit based cabinets for controlled substances, a dispensing robot for most scheduled meds, and an electronic documentation system with a bar code scanner for medications including intravenous solutions.

The benefits of BCMA include the lack of a single medication error for a six-month time period, with an overall increase in patient safety and nursing satisfaction. Much improved charting accuracy and a decrease in the time of overall medication administration has been achieved partly because the computers on wheels can be in or nearly in each patient room with the use of BCMA.

Implementation challenges have included the development and staffing of a system to package doses that provide a bar code label for nursing administration. Pharmacy added about two FTEs for the unit dose bar code packaging and checking process. While some unit dose medication can be purchased with bar codes, a majority of doses need to be pre-packed with a bar code and checked by the pharmacy service. This includes patient specific doses from a busy neonatal service. The safety and time saving advantages of the BCMA clearly have outweighed the challenges of the system.

References

1   Eidem L, Bond J, et al. Evaluation of a point-of-care medication bedside bar code scanning system in a tertiary care teaching hospital. ASHP Midyear Clinical Meeting. 2004; 39(Dec): 237D.

2   Larrabee S, Brown MM. Recognizing the institutional benefits of bar-code point-of-care technology. *Joint Commission Journal on Quality and Safety.* 2003; 29:345–353.

3   Low DK, Belcher JV. Reporting medication errors through computerized medication administration. *Computers, Informatics, Nursing.* 2002; 20:178–83.

4   Anderson S, Wittwer W. Using bar-code point-of-care technology for patient safety. *Journal of Healthcare Quality.* 2004; 26(6):5–11.

5   Center for Information Technology Leadership. The value of computerized provider order entry in ambulatory settings. 2003.

6   Institute of Medicine, Committee on Quality in Healthcare in America. *To Err is Human: Building a Safer Health System.* Washington, DC: National Academies Press; 1999.

Bibliography

Agency for Healthcare Research and Quality. Reducing and preventing adverse drug events to decrease hospital costs. *Research in Action,* Issue 1 (01–0020), Rockville, MD; 2001. http://www.ahcpr.gov/clinic/ptsafety/chap6.htm.

American Nurses Association. Nursing Practice Standards. www.nursingworld.org.

American Society of Health-System Pharmacists. *Best Practices.* Bethesda, MD: 2004–2005 ed. www.ashp.org.

American Society of Health-System Pharmacists. Landmines and Pitfalls of CPOE. http://www.ashp.org/patient-safety/Landmines.cfm?cfid=3389499&CFToken=98144606.

American Society of Health-System Pharmacists Research and Education Foundation. Implementing a Bar Coded Medication Safety Program—Pharmacists Toolkit. Bethesda, MD. http://www.ashpfoundation.org/BarCoded.pdf.

Clark T. CPOE—Medication System Strategy. ASHP Summer Meeting; 2002; 59(Jun); I14.

Field TS. Strategies for detecting adverse drug events among older persons in the ambulatory setting. *J Am Med Inform Assoc.* 2004; Nov–Dec, 11(6):492–498.

HIMSS Bar Coding Task Force. *Implementation Guide for the Use of Bar Code Technology in Healthcare.* Chicago: HIMSS; 2003.

Institute for Safe Medication Practices. Draft Guidelines for Safe Electronic Communication of Medication Orders. www.ismp.org.

Nahm R, Poston I. Measurement of the effects of an integrated, point-of-care computer system on quality of nursing documentation and satisfaction. *Computers in Nursing.* 2000; 18:220–229,

Oren E, Shaffer ER, Guglielmo BJ. Impact of emerging technologies on medication errors and adverse drug events. *Am J Health-Syst Pharm.* 2003; 60(13):1447–1458.

US Pharmacopeia, Inc. [press release]. http://vocuspr.vocus.com/VocusPR30/DotNet/Newsroom/Query.aspx?SiteName=uspnews&Entity=PRAsset&SF_PRAsset_PRAssetID_EQ=95555&XSL=PressRelease&Cache=True.

US Pharmacopia. Dec. 20, 2004 [press release]. http://vocuspr.vocus.com/VocusPR30/DotNet/Newsroom/Query.aspx?SiteName=uspnews&Entity=PRAsset&SF_PRAsset_PRAssetID_EQ=95555&XSL=PressRelease&Cache=True.

CHAPTER 7

Clinical Documentation and Care Planning

Margaret (Peggy) Budnik, DM, RN

Provider organizations are increasingly turning their attention to clinical documentation to improve the efficiency of patient care, provide critical data for clinical decision support, and reduce paper. Improvements in the availability and usability of wireless point of care devices are allowing the process of electronic documentation to be more integrated with the caregiver's workflow. Unlike the implementation of an order management or pharmacy system, the implementation of clinical documentation usually involves a multi-year, phased approach using an admitting assessment form deployed at one point, a pain assessment form at another, and so forth. This chapter highlights the challenges of implementing clinical documentation and the need to have a consistently applied philosophy, structure, and process for the design, implementation, and monitoring of these initiatives.

Clinical documentation is a fundamental component of healthcare practice that includes assessments, case plans, clinical guidelines, and progress notes (see Table 7-1 for EHR standard). In the paper world, the documentation process is relatively stagnant. Over the years, some changes did evolve such as the development of flowcharts and template assessment forms to facilitate the standardization of documentation. However, changing paper forms did not equate to changing the process of documenting care.

Initial efforts at electronic documentation naturally led to automating the existing process—replicating paper forms into an electronic format—even though the old ways of documenting were time consuming and ineffective. As a result, many organizations found that technology alone was not the answer. Old problems resurfaced; new problems

---

Kathy Smith, RN, MS, and Vivienne Smith, RN, BSN, contributed Case Study 8 on Documentation Leverages NANDA/NIC/NOC Classifications. Sherry Phillips-Dykes, BS, RN, contributed Case Study 9 on Clinical Pathways Improve Outcomes.

developed. Solutions were needed, not by replicating the documentation workflow of the past but by defining new processes that crossed all disciplines involved in patient care.

Table 7-1: The HL7 EHR Prescription

Key Functions Specified for Clinical Documentation by the HL7 EHR Standard*	
Manage clinical documents and notes (DC.1.1.6)	Create, addend, correct, authenticate and close, as needed, transcribed or directly-entered clinical documentation and notes.
Support for standard assessments (DC.2.1.1)	Offer prompts to support the adherence to care plans, guidelines, and protocols at the point of information capture.
Manage referrals (DC.1.4.4)	Enable the origination, documentation and tracking of referrals between care providers or healthcare organization, including clinical and administrative details of the referrals.
Support for standard care plans, guidelines, protocols (DC.2.2.1.1)	Support the use of appropriate standard care plans, guidelines, and/or protocols for the management of specific conditions.
Support for context-sensitive care plans, guidelines, protocols (DC.2.2.1.2)	Identify and present the appropriate care plans, guidelines, and/or protocols for the management of specific conditions that are patient-specific.
Capture variances from standard care plans, guidelines, protocols (DC.2.2.1.3)	Identify variances from patient-specific and standard care plans, guidelines, and protocols.
Access Clinical Guidance (DC.2.7.1)	Provide relevant evidence-based information and knowledge to the point of care for use in clinical decisions and care planning.
Manage guidelines, protocols, and patient-specific care plans. (DC.1.2.2)	Provide administrative tools for organizations to build care plans, guidelines, and protocols for use during patient care planning and care.

*For a comprehensive and current list of HL7 EHR standard components, visit www.hl7.org/ehr.

INTERDISCIPLINARY PATIENT CARE

Patient care is not limited to nursing or physician interactions with patients. A number of disciplines are intimately involved in the patient care process. The clinical components each discipline brings to the table may vary; however, each clinician contributes to the overall patient care plan. Nowhere is this more evident than in the EHR.

A common problem in the early stages of design is an over-focus on the data entry aspect of the documentation and how it will impact the sponsoring department; for example, how nurses will document allergies. There is a lack of attention to the bigger picture: the patient's overall plan of care. The whole is greater than the sum of its parts; while each discipline brings vital input to the quality of care, no discipline stands alone. Thus, one of the first steps in designing clinical documentation is defining the professional needs and responsibilities of *all* disciplines involved in or "touched by" the documentation (for allergies this would include physicians and pharmacy at the least). In addition to the questions of what types of data they routinely document, and when the documentation is routinely performed, it is essential to ask also what other disciplines need access to this information, when they need it, whether there a particular "view" of the data that will better integrate it with their workflow, whether they should be able to modify it, and so on.

Even if an organization is just starting to work on clinical documentation, it is essential that an interdisciplinary forum be created. The intent of the EHR should never be to limit the system's functionality at the expense of one department over another. However, decisions should be made collaboratively by representatives from various departments who meet to improve patient care by integrating the EHR. An interdisciplinary committee should include participants from the key clinical departments including nursing, pharmacy, respiratory care, nutrition services, and medical records. These individuals should be knowledgeable about their own specialty and its processes as well have as a good understanding of the big (clinical) picture. The committee should have decision-making authority and a direct link to the appropriate administrative planning/reporting structures. Organizations may also find that there is value in forming smaller interdisciplinary workgroups (e.g., pharmacy and nursing) to facilitate department-specific concerns and issues.

In the paper world, many disciplines find a comfortable gray area where they can work around the rules. In the electronic world, life becomes black and white. It becomes harder (if not impossible) to bend the rules; frustrations can rise and patient care can be compromised. Establishing mechanisms to address issues, conflicts, and protocols together as a team will not only improve clinical documentation, it will also improve the quality of care (Table 7-2).

Table 7-2: The Evidence-Based EHR

Selected Studies Supporting the Benefits of Clinical Documentation	
Nurses perceive EHRs as having the potential to improve patient care and patient safety	A descriptive study of nurse-end users of an EHR documentation system in a large magnet hospital in southwest Florida (representing 23 clinical units) found that the nurses' workload had not increased and that nurses were positive about using an EHR.[1]
Use of information systems increases completeness of nursing assessment and outcome documentation	A study of nursing documentation in a 100-bed urban hospital in Tennessee found that no significant change (improvement) was noticed within the first six months following implementation of their system; however, retraining staff and continued use of the system did improve documentation when measured at 18 months post-implementation.[2]
Nurses spend less time in documentation and more time in patient care	A four-year study in an Australian teaching hospital (intensive care unit) found the implementation of a clinical information system was associated with significant improvements in quality indicators, positive staff perception, and improved nursing recruitment and retention.[3]

DESIGN PROCESS: FOCUS ON WORKFLOW

Designing documentation "forms" in the EHR offers new opportunities for charting. Options include template-driven formats that "walk" users through standard questions. Templates typically offer prompts and clinical choices that can be invaluable aids to the staff, particularly inexperienced personnel who may need extra guidance in appropriate documentation.

Users should be involved in the design portion of building documentation screens, as they will be more likely to accept a system when they are intimately involved and able to determine what processes and aspects of their workflow will need to be redesigned to leverage the system. They will understand (and help communicate) not only the changes coming, but also the rationales behind the change.

EHR users may find that something that made sense in the design phase may not work as planned post-implementation. The key to a successful implementation is flexibility. The design process can either enhance or impede not only documentation, but also the delivery of care.

THE CHALLENGES OF "COLLECT ONCE, REUSE MANY"

One of the most beneficial yet risky opportunities of electronic clinical documentation is the sharing and re-use of information. Collecting the information once and re-using it many times enhances patient care, safety and satisfaction. Data re-use is also one of the most attractive features of the EHR for busy caregivers as it reduces redundant documentation, freeing time for direct care activities. However, while the concept is inviting, the outcome could be disastrous if not implemented with planning, education, and caution.

Data that carry over from one visit to another can be termed "patient historic data"; examples are a list of patient allergies, a list of current medications, or a notification of isolation needs. This type of data ensures continuity of care; it also provides immediate visibility to previously identified needs/conditions that could expedite care in subsequent encounters. If a patient is readmitted, a list of allergies, a list of home (current) medications, or special isolation needs would be immediately available to the care provider seeing the patient.

A similar function is "visit historic data" where data can be carried over from one clinical note to another within the same visit, for example, nursing shift assessments. This functionality can be a valuable tool in settings where users chart by exception. The last documented status displays in the new event for the current user to review and update. If there is no change in the patient status, the user can "accept" the note as it appears. However, if the patient's status changes, the user has the ability (and the professional responsibility) to update the note to reflect the patient's current condition.

The problem is that users often find that it is so easy to accept the information already in the system that they do not update for changes when they do occur. As a result, inaccurate data may become part of the patient's record. This problem cannot totally be placed at the doorstep of the users as their workload and the acuity of their patients continues to escalate. In the electronic world, pressure is put on caregivers to "clear" their work list. Focus can shift from valuing what was documented to completing all scheduled events.

The solution can be simple—if the involved parties work together in identifying problems and implementing solutions. Any new functionality, such as the use of historic data, needs to be communicated to the users. Education (and possibly re-education) on general documentation principles, as well as the use of the new tools, must be provided. Finally, monitor – monitor – monitor, not only through the implementation process, but as an ongoing initiative that is incorporated into ongoing peer evaluation efforts. Table 7-3 provides a summary of important considerations for EHR implementation.

Table 7-3: Clinical Documentation Implementation Considerations

☑ Adopt organizational philosophy: EHR implementation is less about technology and more about change management.
☑ Foster multidisciplinary and interdisciplinary involvement throughout the process: Communication and participation are the keys to success.
☑ Implement in phases, piloting changes and new initiatives first: Much is learned "when the rubber meets the road."
☑ Prepare system downtime procedures including what will be backloaded after the downtime.
☑ Look for opportunities to reduce redundancy, improve information sharing, and ensure proper updating.
☑ Use standard clinical terminology where possible.
☑ Audit compliance with documentation standards electronically through reports that measure the timeliness of documentation and other compliance indicators.
☑ Integrate (with clinicians) workflow and change process to improve compliance and efficiencies.
☑ Capture charges as a by-product of documentation.
☑ Ensure that downstream uses of data for viewing, clinical decision support and reporting are considered.
☑ Involve medical records staff to ensure compliance with Legal Medical Record standards (see Chapter 12).
☑ Honor and do not try to replace the caregiver's critical thinking skills.

POINT-OF-CARE AND CLINICAL DEVICE INTERFACES

Another method of facilitating documentation is interfacing clinical systems. Building interfaces between monitoring devices and clinical information systems can save clinicians valuable time—time that could be spent with patients. One common interface is the automatic download of blood glucose results taken with a hand-held glucometer at the patient's bedside. Instead of measuring the patient's glucose level and then "manually" entering the results on paper or in the EHR, the device sends data directly to the EHR via a docking station or wireless connection that can transmit the data into the patient's record and automatically post a note and pass a charge. Direct EHR to device interfaces are also available for collecting data from hemodynamic monitoring devices in critical care or emergency room settings where patients may be physiologically unstable and require frequent monitoring. System users and IT analysts must remember to look beyond the obvious benefits of these new tools and remember to always search for potential utilization issues that may impact patient care, for example, inaccurate data transmission and documentation.

One basic philosophy should be adopted by all EHR users: the clinical information system is not the licensed professional. Technology is a tool. It may become more sophisticated and clinicians may become more dependent on its functionality, but at the end of the day, caregivers are ultimately responsible for the quality of care given and for the quality of the documentation in the EHR. Machines may learn to communicate with one another; they may even be programmed to identify potential risks and interactions. However, the ultimate responsibility for critical thinking and caring for patients remains in the heart and soul of the caregiver.

CLINICAL GUIDELINES AND PATHWAYS

Clinical guidelines can be defined as a means of ensuring that practice is evidence-based. Guidelines play an integral role in delivering quality care in an efficient, consistent, and cost-effective manner. However, simply because guidelines exist, organizations cannot assume that they will automatically be used. The challenge at hand is to create a successful implementation process in which guidelines are turned into actions—actions that will influence decision-making behaviors and encourage clinicians to change their practice. The EHR can play a pivotal role in the incorporation of guidelines into practice.

Implementing guidelines can be a complex process, whether introduced on paper or electronically. Regardless of the format, communication is critical to user acceptance. Clinicians need to understand the goals of the protocols and how using the guidelines may impact their roles in delivering care. The expertise and judgment that each clinician brings to the patient must be recognized. The introduction of guidelines should not devalue the clinician's knowledge and experience; rather, guidelines should give clinicians more time to do what they do best—care for their patients.

The EHR opens the door to new opportunities in facilitating the development and utilization of clinical pathways. While the process of designing clinical pathways in the paper world was relatively successful in many organizations, they were often difficult to convert into practice. Success depended on human intervention. Incorporating the paper design into the electronic record is possible. The electronic record's advantage is the use of computerized logic, which automatically translates the plan into actions as specific pre-defined criteria are met.

The process of implementing clinical pathways closely mirrors the steps previously discussed. However, one important feature must be considered in the planning/design phase. The outcomes—criteria that determine the patient's progress along the pathway—must be measurable. In the paper world, the human user has the ability to translate less objective criteria and make clinical decisions. Clinical systems deal with absolutes, that is, clearly defined objective criteria. Therefore, the design phase in implementing clinical pathways requires special attention to defining the pathway progression in objective terms.

CONSIDERING THE NEEDS OF DOWNSTREAM USERS

The initial implementation of an EHR traditionally focuses on the actual documentation process—that is, entering data into the clinical system. Regardless of the discipline, clinicians focus on "how" to best get the data into the system. If the process is too cumbersome or time consuming, users will resist using the system.

The EHR provides an opportunity to create role-specific "views" of the chart for users, thus enhancing data retrieval. For example, in the paper world, a respiratory therapist may need to refer to several areas of the chart to find all the information needed to determine what therapy is needed and document it. In the EHR, a "Respiratory Therapist View" filters out the data that is not relevant and allows the therapist to focus on what is pertinent. Views of the data created through clinical documentation should be considered as part of the design process to ensure that what is documented is used effectively.

In addition to online displays of clinical information, the EHR provides the opportunity to improve concurrent data collection for reporting and analysis. When designing documentation, users should consider what information they will need to retrieve. The demands of regulatory agencies and voluntary participation in various quality benchmark initiatives have also heightened the importance of data retrieval from the EHR. One of the most important forms of data retrieval to consider is the actual chart print. Chapter 12 on the Legal Health Record addresses these issues. Other emerging trending related to clinical documentation are provided in Table 7-4.

CHARGE CAPTURE

Clinical documentation can also be leveraged to improve an organization's bottom line by reducing missed or lost charges. Capturing charges in the paper world is not traditionally associated with clinical documentation. Charting patient care is one thing; completing charge slips is another. The EHR offers the opportunity for users to chart "what" happened to a patient from a clinical perspective and have the documentation automatically post a charge.

Some departments have historically done a better job capturing charges, especially departments that are order/result oriented, such as radiology or laboratory. For each procedure performed, an associated charge can be generated. This process translates very well into the EHR. However, the real benefit in the EHR can be realized for less procedurally-oriented departments. For example, when documenting chest tube outputs or enteral feeding assessments, nurses can easily answer a question: was the container/bag changed/replaced? Pre-built charges can be generated as part of the routine nursing note.

Once again, getting buy-in from the user community is critical. Users who do not typically associate their clinical documentation with charges appreciate the opportunity to simplify the process. Rather than documenting their note and then having to complete a charge slip, both transactions can be consolidated into a single activity.

All healthcare workers are aware of the financial constraints being experienced by the industry. As a result, communication of successful outcomes from charge capture initiatives should be shared with the staff. This communication not only acknowledges the positive change being realized, it also encourages users to participate in the process by identifying new ways of capturing additional charges.

Table 7-4: Three-Year Prognosis: Clinical Documentation

✳ Increased utilization of standardization of clinical vocabulary and classifications.
✳ Increasing integration of medical monitoring devices to directly document clinical information.
✳ Continuing evolution of portable device evolution and tailoring to the specific needs of the clinician.
✳ Development of structured methods for creating progress notes

Case Study 8: Documentation Leverages NANDA/NIC/NOC Classifications

Organization:	University of Colorado Hospital, Denver, Colorado
Acute Care Facilities:	1
Staffed Beds:	450
Type:	Academic Medical Center

Hospitals struggle to demonstrate evidence of interdisciplinary care planning. Often, there is a lack of information-sharing among disciplines, resulting in various types of inefficiencies and delays of services. However, electronic documentation, using standardized terminology, provides the opportunity for clinicians to efficiently communicate the plan of care, as well as patient status, in relation to identified goals and outcomes.

A group of clinicians at the University of Colorado Hospital (UCH) was convened to develop a plan to reach this goal. The group decided to introduce the standard classification systems of NANDA (North American Nursing Diagnosis Association, NIC (Nursing Interventions Classification), and NOC (Nursing Outcomes Classification) to describe the process of problem identification, care planning, patient care, and outcome measurement. After extensive development of clinical content and screen customization, clinicians were able to use the order entry application to construct the care plan. Nurses would assess the patient and identify patient problems using NANDA. Next, appropriate NICs were entered as nursing orders, replacing the paper Kardex. Patient care was electronically documented, linking orders to related elements of the care plan.

During the building phase, various disciplines provided input. Screens were standardized based on input from the clinical experts, using evidence-based standards of practice. It became clear that NIC would be a good fit for multiple clinical specialties. As a result, other disciplines were integrated into the new system. The end result was the construction of an interdisciplinary care plan that identified problems, goals, interventions, and outcomes.

In the end, the patients reaped the benefits from this project. The entire professional care plan was centrally located and organized within a standard framework of terminology. The plan enhanced communication, which facilitated teamwork. A mechanism was established to track a patient's progress from initial problem identification through intervention and outcome measurement.

Case Study 9: Clinical Pathways Improve Outcomes

Organization:	Forrest General Hospital, Hattiesburg, Mississippi
Acute Care Facilities:	1
Staffed Beds:	550
Type:	Community Hospital

Caregivers must pull from multiple knowledge bases to determine best practices for patients. As a result, a project was initiated to improve efficiency and quality by implementing online clinical guidelines. To date, 53 clinical pathways have been automated.

A Performance Improvement Team was formed per diagnosis, each chaired by a physician. Each group researched best practices, established benchmark facilities, developed order sets, and defined discharge criteria and patient outcomes. The pathways were piloted on paper prior to electronic implementation.

The process is simple. Pathway orders are initiated when a patient with a predefined pathway diagnosis is admitted. Additional orders from the admitting physician are also addressed; however, use of the pathway orders automatically triggers ancillary referrals at the time of admission. A plan of care, including outcomes and goals, is initiated without waiting for human intervention. Outcomes are reviewed and updated every shift by nursing and other disciplines. All caregivers are able to review the patient's plan and status easily in the EHR, especially since deviations can easily be spotted due to color coding the variations in the electronic display. Clinical pathways can follow patients across the continuum of care (acute to outpatient) or can be resolved at any point in time, depending on the patient's needs.

Challenges were encountered during the implementation phase, including physician resistance, staff not ordering the entire phase of the pathway, staff forgetting to process variances, and staff not resolving the pathways at discharge. However, benefits were also realized, including:

- Improved efficiency (time saved from not having to write plans of care as well as easier order entry process);
- Automatic multidisciplinary care plan initiated;
- Automatic education reminders generated;
- Improved patient outcomes with decreased cost and length of stay; and
- Improved access to aggregate outcome data for quality improvement.

References

1   Moody LE, Slocumb E, Berg B, Jackson D. Electronic health records documentation in nursing: Nurses' perceptions, attitudes and preferences. *CIN: Computers, Informatics, Nursing.* 2004; 22(6):337–344.

2   Larrabee JH, Boldreghini S, Elder-Sorrells K, et al. Evaluation of documentation before and after implementation of a nursing information system in an acute care hospital. *CIN: Computers, Informatics, Nursing.* 2001; 19(2):56–65.

3   Fraenkel BM, Cowie M, Daley P. Quality benefits of an intensive care clinical information system. *Critical Care Medicine.* 2003; 31(1):120–125.

CHAPTER 8

Clinical Decision Support

Jerome A. Osheroff, MD, FACP, FACMI, and Joe Miller, MA, FHIMSS

The greatest value of the EHR is realized when it includes clinical decision support (CDS): embedded clinical knowledge that helps users appropriately gather, interpret, and respond to EHR data and provide the highest quality patient care. Some types of CDS, such as reference materials that users can access to answer questions about drug therapy or condition management, are relatively straightforward to integrate into EHRs and can be attempted early in implementation. Other CDS interventions that might be more disruptive to workflow or require rich EHR data are best attempted after the EHR, and organizational processes to manage CDS content, are solidly in place. While elements of CDS have been discussed in earlier sections, this chapter highlights some overarching considerations for effectively deploying CDS in the EHR.

EHRs are powerful tools not only for managing patient data and clinical processes but also for delivering knowledge to clinicians to help ensure that the data, and information about best clinical practices, are used appropriately in patient management. CDS interventions are best deployed as part of a systematic program aimed at achieving the healthcare organization's well-defined objectives of importance. These targets might include decreasing medication errors or supporting disease management initiatives, among many others. Effective CDS programs include determining goals with key stakeholders; evaluating EHR and related information system capabilities for delivering knowledge interventions; developing, validating, and launching the interventions;

Terri Andrews, RN, MBA, contributed Case Study 10 on Clinical Alerts Improve Performance. Lynn Sund, RN, MS, MBA, contributed Case Study 11 on Nursing Rules Enhance Skin Management.

evaluating their effects; and repeating the process in a continuous improvement cycle. These steps are discussed in detail in the book, *Improving Outcomes with Clinical Decision Support: An Implementer's Guide.*[1] This chapter highlights some specific considerations for implementing CDS in EHRs. Table 8-1 provides key HL7 EHR standard requirements for CDS.

CDS is the lever that rests on the EHR fulcrum and has the capability to lift enormous value for the organization and its patients. The value of CDS for patient safety and clinical outcomes is well established, and the benefits for operational efficiency can be extensive. In fact, such knowledge delivery is the foundation for achieving many key EHR benefits related to safer, higher quality, and more cost-effective patient care. As government and private payers move toward a pay-for-performance approach to reimbursement, CDS will become an essential tool in implementing and monitoring the performance improvements needed to meet the standards.

Table 8-1: The HL7 EHR Prescription

Key Functions Specified for Clinical Decision Support by the HL7 EHR Standard*	
Support for standard assessments (DC.2.1.1)	Offer prompts to support the adherence to care plans, guidelines, and protocols at the point of information capture.
Support for patient context-enabled assessments (DC.2.1.2)	Offer prompts based on patient-specific data at the point of information capture.
Support for identification of potential problems and trends (DC.2.1.3)	Identify trends that may lead to significant problems and provide prompts for consideration.
Support for patient and family preferences (DC.2.1.4)	Support the integration of patient and family preferences into clinical decision support at all appropriate opportunities.
Support for drug interaction checking (DC.2.3.1.1)	Identify drug interaction warnings at the point of medication ordering.
Patient specific dosing and warnings (DC.2.3.1.2)	Identify and present appropriate dose recommendations based on patient-specific conditions and characteristics at the time of medication ordering.

* For a comprehensive and current list of HL7 EHR standard components, visit www.hl7.org/ehr.

The planning and introduction of CDS interventions is one of the most organizationally challenging elements of EHR implementation. Fundamentally, EHR implementation is about the efficient collecting and sharing of clinical information and then adapting care processes to accommodate these new data management approaches. Such changes alone certainly can be complex. However, CDS more fundamentally affects clinical decisions and thus requires additional attention to a host of other issues as well. For example, some clinicians can view certain CDS interventions as a challenge to their clinical judgment and autonomy. A systematic approach to CDS deployment, distinct from but closely related to EHR deployment, can be helpful in ensuring that the CDS program effectively achieves its goals (Table 8-2).

Table 8-2: The Evidence-Based EHR: Selected Studies Supporting the Benefits of Clinical Decision Support

CDS patient safety opportunities supported by evidence[2]	Lists 11 patient safety practices that were the most highly rated (of the 79 practices reviewed in detail) in terms of strength of the evidence supporting more widespread implementation.
Physician performance[3]	68 studies on CDS impact were reviewed, finding that CDS can enhance clinical performance for drug dosing, preventive care, and other aspects of medical care, but not convincingly for diagnosis.
Medication safety[4]	13 studies reviewed indicating that CDS can substantially reduce medication error rates.
Chronic care management[5]	CDS is valuable in care management for four chronic diseases (asthma, depression, diabetes, and congestive heart failure) that result in 170,000 U.S. deaths annually.

TYPES OF CDS INTERVENTION DECISION SUPPORT

There are a variety of ways that clinical knowledge can be imbedded as CDS interventions within EHRs. These include care documentation templates, condition-specific data flow sheets, order sets, protocols and pathways, integrated clinical references, and alerts and reminders. These CDS interventions can be used in several of the EHR subsystems, such as order entry, results review, laboratory and pharmacy systems. For example, pharmacy systems might contain links to detailed information and alerts about preparing medications and avoiding drug interactions to help pharmacists ensure that medications are delivered safely.

Some consider CDS synonymous with alerts and reminders, but a broader perspective that utilizes the full spectrum of knowledge delivery opportunities provides a much richer toolkit for bringing about the desired improvements in care. For example, providing an alert that a patient has not received an indicated medication after an order entry session might be less efficient than providing information about appropriate practice farther upstream in the care process. In this case, an order set might save the clinician time at order entry and make it easier to put the patient on the appropriate medications in the first place. *Improving Outcomes with Clinical Decision Support*[1] provides detailed guidance on selecting specific CDS interventions and opportunities in clinical workflow for achieving specific objectives.

In many EHR implementations, alerts related to detecting adverse drug events (ADEs) will be a key initial foray into CDS. These rules check a medication order against patient allergies, dosing standards, and drug-drug interactions and can be an important element of medication safety programs. These CDS interventions have been common in pharmacy systems for some time, but additional deployment and use issues come into play when they are incorporated in point-of-care applications such as CPOE. Doctors and nurses may be less tolerant of excessive "noise" from these interventions, that is, the proportion of alerts that might not be pertinent for one reason or another to the patient at hand. This noise can result from a variety of factors, including inadequate data available to the "rule," when this data would have indicated that the alert is not appropriate in specific cases.

Other rules besides medication checking may be used by the organization and deployed via a rules "engine" that is part of the EHR. The same attention to the noise from these rules is required. Components of rules to consider include:

- Rule Trigger: The EHR event that that is monitored by the rule. This could be an order being entered, a form being saved, or other activity. The event can be initiated by the user, but might also include EHR initiated actions such as the posting of a laboratory result.
- Rule Logic: The rule monitors EHR activity for the trigger(s) and evaluates a logical, or 'IF…THEN…'" expression to determine if a specific action should result. For example, a rule might monitor the patient problem list for conditions that require specific drug therapy. The rule logic might state, "IF patient has disease X, and is not on medication Y, THEN send an alert to the clinician."
- Rule Action or Message: When the trigger conditions cause a rule to fire, and the logic conditions are met, a specific action results. In many cases this is a message to someone involved in caring for the patient. Effective alerts to clinicians should include the rationale for the alert (e.g., citations to the evidence base supporting the recommendation), as well as some mechanism for taking the recommended action (e.g., ordering the recommended drug).

Table 8-3 provides several basic examples of CDS rules.

Table 8-3: CDS Rule Examples

Trigger	Logic	Action/Message
Physician or pharmacist enters medication order.	Series of rules fires to check the medication against the patient's allergies, other drugs currently ordered, pertinent lab values, age, and body mass index.	Immediate online alert warns the user of allergy conflict. User can change the medication or override the alert.
A field on an online nursing assessment form is marked to indicate that the patient uses oxygen at home.	When the form is completed and electronically signed, a rule checks whether this field indicates home oxygen use.	An order is created by the system for a respiratory consult and a task is placed on the work list of the appropriate respiratory therapist.
Patient is admitted as an in-patient.	A rule fires checking if the patient was recorded as having a methicillin-resistant infection during a previous encounter.	A printout is generated in the infection control department and a precaution flag is set on the patient's online profile for this encounter.

Other powerful CDS interventions deployed in EHRs include order sets and more sophisticated patient care guidelines and pathways, as discussed in earlier chapters. These interventions leverage the workflow and data management capabilities of the EHR to help clinicians implement high-quality, consistent care plans that are based on the best available evidence and practice standards.

Other CDS intervention types exert less direct influence over care decisions, but nonetheless play an important role in supporting appropriate data gathering, documentation, and analysis. These include documentation templates that help ensure that nurses, physicians, and other clinicians with direct patient contact gather and document all the information needed to fully inform decision-making. These data can also be important for reimbursement purposes and to provide triggers needed for rule-based CDS interventions. Data flow sheets, which aggregate all the information pertinent to a particular condition, can similarly be useful in helping clinicians identify important patterns and in ensuring clinical decisions are informed by the appropriate data.

EHR systems are becoming more sophisticated in the mechanisms they offer for deploying the various types of CDS interventions. Increasingly, products have the more standard CDS interventions embedded, reducing the programming effort needed to drive the intervention. Infobuttons, which provide context-sensitive links to reference information, are a good example of this. EHRs are increasingly providing Infobutton functionality, that is, hyperlinks placed next to EHR content such as names of drugs and clinical problems that take the user directly to the point in online references providing information specifically about that item. Infobuttons deployed in EHRs will increasingly be capable of sending patient specific data (e.g., age, kidney function information, other illnesses) that will further tune the linked information to the patient-specific circumstances.

Despite the increasing sophistication of CDS functionality in EHRs, it should be reiterated that a primary challenge with CDS generally is not the technical implementation but rather the organizational priority setting for CDS objectives and the change management efforts needed to ensure that the CDS interventions achieve the objectives.

EHR PREREQUISITES FOR CDS

It can be easier to introduce new CDS interventions, particularly those that involve significant changes to practice or workflow, as the EHR deployment stabilizes and matures in the organization. While many useful CDS interventions require relatively little EHR data (e.g., documentation templates and Infobuttons), others (such as certain rules) may require a critical mass of EHR data to be optimally useful. In any case, it is desirable for EHR users to already be comfortable with EHR workflow capabilities, such as work lists, so that they are not overloaded with all the new skills required to interact effectively with both the new EHR system and with too many new and complex CDS interventions.

Table 8-4 lists the types of EHR clinical and administrative information that can be particularly useful when developing alerts. There are many CDS interventions that will work with a limited amount of information, but even a seemingly simple rule can require a wide array of data to be most effective. For example, an organization that wants to reduce falls might want to implement a CDS rule to discourage the prescribing of a specific sedative class to elderly patients. The rule could be triggered whenever a drug from this class is prescribed to a patient over age 65.

An alert based on this information alone would likely create many "false positives" and be viewed as a nuisance to the caregiver. With additional information such as the patient's location, documentation of fall precautions, pain assessments, problem list, and so on, the alert can be honed to more specifically target clinicians in whom it will be most useful and least annoying. In general, the more pertinent data that can be brought to bear in triggering an alert and informing its logic, the fewer false positives will result. This, in turn, increases the likelihood that the recipient will appreciate the alert message and that the rule will have the desired effect.

Table 8-4: EHR Prerequisite Data to Support Alerts

Information	Common Uses
Laboratory results	Used for checking for renal function when ordering drugs eliminated by or toxic to the kidney. Alerting of critical laboratory values.
Medications	Allergy checking, dose range checking, drug-drug interactions.
Orders	Checking for duplicate or inappropriate therapy. Orders can also be used as a surrogate indicator of the patient's clinical problems for CDS purposes when formal problem list documentation is not available in appropriate format for this purpose.
Admission, discharge and transfer	Many rules are more effective if qualified by patient type (inpatient, outpatient, etc.), location or unit type (ICU, maternity, etc.) and other ADT information.
Caregivers	Identify which caregiver should get asynchronous alerts such as work list entries or an e-mail. Note that keeping track of who is the primary caregiver, either physician or nurse, at any given time is complex and often not handled to the level of accuracy that is required by CDS interventions.
Encounter history	The ability to check when and for what the patient was last admitted is useful in rules that fire at the time of admission.
Clinical documentation	Among the most valuable for rules are: • assessments • allergies • problems • precautions • patient preference

Table 8-5: Key Stakeholders for CDS Interventions

Stakeholder	Description
Change agent	May be the performance improvement department or operational areas that are charged with, or have assumed the role of getting the organization to move toward a more evidenced-based or efficient approach to delivering care.
Clinical leadership	The department head or other clinical leaders in the area where the CDS interventions are likely to occur. For example, an order set for suspected MI should be developed or validated with input from the cardiology chair and department.
Data collectors and owners	CDS often relies on upstream data collectors/owners who may need to change how or when they acquire data needed for the intervention. For example, a rule that depends on data from an admission assessment may require that nursing complete the assessment earlier in the admission than was previously acceptable.
Workflow-affected caregivers	The CDS intervention will impact workflow for one or more stakeholders; these individuals need to be well represented in CDS development and deployment to ensure they respond appropriately to the intervention.

IMPLEMENTATION ISSUES

Below are some issues to keep in mind when setting up a CDS program and implementing CDS interventions.

Stakeholder Involvement

An essential first step in establishing a CDS program involves identifying the key individuals, committees and positions whose enthusiastic commitment, or at least tacit support, is required for the CDS interventions. Table 8-5 lists some types of stakeholders who should be involved in the CDS effort. Typically some combination of these stakeholders is involved in a CDS steering committee that oversees and coordinates CDS-related activities in the organization. This committee is generally connected to some key organizational governing body.

"Rules Fix Everything" Fallacy

In some organizations there is a tendency to view rules as a panacea for getting clinicians to comply with established procedures. This overdependence on rules can divert attention from the real problem that might be handled more appropriately with improved training, support, and monitoring. Remember to consider the full spectrum of available CDS interventions for achieving specific goals, and utilize alerts only as most appropriate.

Alert Overload

As discussed above, a common problem with alerts is that they can produce a large number of "false positives" that frustrate users and result in a large number of alert overrides. This is often the case because the rule does not have access to sufficient data in the EHR to determine if an intervention is appropriate or not. Judicious use of alerts only when they are the most appropriate intervention, honing alert triggers and logic, and carefully vetting alerts with stakeholders before launch can help minimize alert overload. Also, monitor the level of alert overrides with aggregate reports. Rules that are being overridden with greater frequency than expected are candidates for review and tuning. Improved tools for reducing alert overload are expected as vendor products mature. See Table 8-6 for other emerging trends related to decision support.

Workflow Integration

Almost by definition, CDS interventions alter clinician workflow and require its careful attention and appropriate response. Extensively involving those who will be affected by the interventions in their development can help optimize integration into workflow and user acceptance. After launch, educating intended CDS recipients in their proper use is a key success ingredient.

Coordination across Information Systems

The EHR in most facilities comprises multiple systems, each of which may have their own CDS capabilities. It is important that CDS content is consistent across the systems. For example, drug dosing information presented in reference information and alerts in pharmacy, nursing, and CPOE systems should all be consistent. Similarly, if the lab system uses a different method of calculating creatinine clearance than the pharmacy system, CDS interventions based on this calculation may be inconsistent and confuse caregivers.

Coordination across Clinical Areas

CDS is often approached locally, that is, one department may wish to implement interventions to accomplish objectives pertinent to that department. However, it is often the case that an issue that appears local to a department actually has broader implications across the organization. In general, CDS should be approached from an organization-wide perspective, both in assessing the needs and in developing and deploying the interventions.

The information presented in this chapter provides a brief overview of selected issues pertinent to CDS implementation in EHRs. Readers are encouraged to consult *Improving Outcomes with Clinical Decision Support: An Implementer's Guide*[1] for more detailed guidance on setting up a successful CDS program.

Table 8-6: Three-Year Prognosis: Clinical Decision Support

☑ Organizations implementing EHRs will approach CDS in a more systematic fashion, as a means to achieving specific objectives of key importance to the organization.

☑ Regulatory, reimbursement, and certifying organizations such as CMS, CCHIT and JCAHO increasingly will expect organizations to effectively utilize CDS interventions to meet their care delivery standards.

☑ EHR and CDS vendors will offer increasingly richer content and tools for deploying CDS interventions and achieving their desired objectives.

☑ Improved tools for increasing the signal to noise ratio of alerts and integrating them into caregiver workflow will evolve.

Case Study 10: Clinical Alerts Improve Performance

Organization:	Alamance Regional Medical Center, Burlington, North Carolina
Acute Care Facilities:	1
Staffed Beds:	238
Type:	Community Hospital

Alamance Regional Medical Center (ARMC), a 238-bed community hospital, was a pioneer for the early adoption of CPOE. With the implementation of its clinical information system in 1998, ARMC has proven that advanced clinical information systems can truly help healthcare organizations increase patient safety through the use of clinical decision support. The organization is currently live with CPOE, results reporting, nursing flow sheets, the electronic medical administration record, and clinical decision support.

With over 75 clinical alerts in place, ARMC can provide its clinicians with real-time information at the point of decision-making utilizing decision support capability. Through the use of CDS, ARMC has successfully addressed a number of organizational issues. The ARMC rules engine uses Arden Syntax and has the ability to produce synchronous or asynchronous alerts. The alerts can come in the form of an e-mail alert, alphanumeric pager alert, or as an alert populating an alerts column in the clinical information system. Below are examples:

Digital Echo Usage
Challenge: Digital Echo usage for Medicare patients was high, putting ARMC in the 97th percentile for hospitals.
Alert: Alert physician at the time of order entry when a digital echo has been performed within the last six months.
Outcome: Digital Echo usage dropped dramatically to the 48th percentile within three months.

Transfusion Criteria

Challenge: Lab manually reviewed only a subset of transfusions for appropriateness and followed up on outliers up to three months later.

Alert: Alert physician online at time of transfusion order when initial transfusion criteria have not been met. The alert box prompts the physician to select a coded reason for the transfusion criteria override.

Outcome: Ninety percent of physicians who see the alert give a coded response real time, reducing amount of outlier follow-up, improving quality of explanations, and allowing 100% of the transfusions to be reviewed.

Maximum Acetaminophen

Challenge: Pharmacy was concerned with patients receiving too much Acetaminophen in a 24-hour period (>=4,000mg). This was difficult to monitor due to the fact that there are many Acetaminophen-containing drugs in the formulary, each containing varying amounts.

Alert: Calculate total Acetaminophen when the nurse documents dose using the EMAR, and alert pharmacy if >=4,000 mg.

Outcome: Pharmacy aware of patients with potential liver damage. Able to intervene and reduce amount of Acetaminophen patient is receiving.

STAT Medications

Challenge: Physicians concerned that STAT medications were not being administered fast enough.

Alert: Send pager message to Charge Nurse when STAT medication ordered.

Outcome: Average medication administration time reduced from 40 to 17 minutes.

Putting a structure in place to support the introduction of clinical decision support capability is key to its success. Educating clinicians to think of alerts when they are trying to solve problems is critical. What might seem impossible to do in a paper world is often very simple with a computer. Requests for alerts come from many different sources and have included pharmacy, the Infection Control Committee, physicians, nursing and ancillary staff.

The Physician Review Board (PRB) serves as the clearinghouse for alerts that impact the physician community. The PRB is composed of physicians representing the different specialties and has been instrumental in representing the physician perspective in the design and implementation of the clinical information system. The PRB physicians often serve as testers of an alert prior to it being placed in production. There is a similar structure in place through the Clinical Informatics Council that represents the nursing and ancillary staffs.

Finally, an organization can achieve success with clinical decision support only if the physicians and clinicians find the alerts to be of value. Be mindful of creating too many alerts, as this will overwhelm the clinicians with the ultimate outcome being alerts that are ignored. Listen to the feedback provided by clinicians and reevaluate if the alert is truly having a positive impact on patient care. Periodically reviewing the alert to see if it is still valued or relevant is important.

Case Study 11: Nursing Rules Enhance Skin Management

Organization:	St. Francis Hospital, Tulsa, Oklahoma
Acute Care Facilities:	1
Staffed Beds:	900
Type:	Community Hospital

The prevalence of pressure ulcers is a key nursing sensitive quality indicator at St. Francis Hospital. The Skin Management Committee assumed the challenge of improving the clinical outcomes associated with pressure ulcers in 2003. The committee decided to use the rules engine of the clinical system to help the nurses better manage and track the skin assessments and nursing interventions that directly impacted skin integrity, specifically the development of pressure ulcers. The change process included evidence-based research as well as incorporating the new standards into the hospital's policies. The clinical database was customized to accommodate the new guidelines.

When the skin assessment (Braden Risk Scale) is electronically documented in the EHR, the system "reads" the patient's risk level (and the presence of any documented ulcers). Based on the pre-built rules (as defined in the revised policy), the system automatically orders and schedules the appropriate skin reassessments and nursing interventions. The nurse is prompted to assess the patient and document the appropriate interventions throughout the hospitalization. An entry into the electronic plan of care is also automatically generated, giving other care providers visibility of the patient's needs and status. This plan of care changes as different rules are met.

After 12 months, the findings were impressive. For five years, the hospital averaged a prevalence rate of 16% (statistically comparable with the national average). Following the nursing decision support initiative, the prevalence rate for pressure ulcers decreased by 57% in 2004, falling to the 7th percentile.

The facility has since expanded the use of criteria-driven orders, reminders, and management queues to various other nursing initiatives. Users continue to witness how decision support can improve quality, promote patient safety, and make the day-to-day workload just a little easier on the bedside nurse.

References

1   Osheroff JA, Pifer EA, Teich JM, Sittig DF, Jenders RA. *Improving Outcomes with Clinical Decision Support: An Implementer's Guide.* Chicago: HIMSS; 2005.

2   Agency for Healthcare Research and Quality. *Making Health Care Safer: A Critical Analysis of Patient Safety Practices.* July 2001. http://www.ahrq.gov/clinic/ptsafety/summrpt.htm. (See especially the 11 practices strongly supported by evidence and Chapter 53, Clinical decision support systems.)

3   Hunt DL, Haynes RB, Hanna SE, Smith K. Effects of computer-based clinical decision support systems on physician performance and patient outcomes: a systematic review. *JAMA.* 1998; 280(15):1339–1346. (See Tables 1-3 for outcomes measured and effects.)

SECTION III

INFORMATION SHARING

CHAPTER 9

Patient-Provider E-Communication and Portals

Eric M. Liederman, MD, MPH, Daniel Z. Sands, MD, MPH, FACMI, and Matt Handley, MD

Over the past 30 years the focus of the EHR has been on providing accurate and timely information to clinicians delivering care. As patients seek to become partners in the process of delivering healthcare and wellness, they are increasingly demanding access to their own clinical information and the ability to communicate electronically with their caregivers. In addition, the Office of the National Coordinator of Health Information Technology's Framework for Strategic Action highlights patient electronic access to their health records as a key strategy. This creates a whole new dynamic and set of requirements for the EHR. This chapter explores the current state and potential of Internet-based healthcare access by patients.

PATIENTS ACCESSING SELF-HELP RESOURCES ONLINE

Internet use has exploded in recent years. Sixty-nine percent of Americans have Internet access from work or home[1] including 58% of 55- to 64-year-olds and 22% of those 65 and older.[2] Historically marginalized groups are also catching up quickly: 53% of the uninsured, 59% of Hispanics, 43% of African-Americans, and 44% of those making less than $30,000 a year are online.[3,4]

Americans increasingly access online self-help healthcare services. Seventy-four percent use the Internet to research medical information,[1] including 19% of persons who are indigent.[5] Consumers in most states can go beyond information research to bypass their doctor and order their own laboratory tests and radiology studies.[6] Patients connect online in support groups[7] and refill prescriptions at their pharmacy's or HMO's Web site.

Many Americans (42%) keep personal health records; 5% do so electronically, primarily to provide doctors with useful information, to recall the care they received, and to access in an emergency and while traveling.[8,9] The federal government has called for the development of electronic PHRs,[10] which are currently available at fee-based

Web sites and as portable technology, such as specially configured USB flash memory drives.[11] The HL7 EHR functions relevant to electronic patient-provider communication are presented in Table 9-1.

Table 9-1: The HL7 EHR Prescription

Key Functions Specified for Patient-Provider Communication by the HL7 EHR Standard*	
Provider and patient or family communication (DC.3.2.3)	Trigger or respond to electronic communication (inbound and outbound) between providers and patients or patient representatives with pertinent actions in the care process.
Patient, family and caregiver education (DC.3.2.4)	Identify and make available electronically or in print any educational or support resources for patients, families, and caregivers that are most pertinent for a given health concern, condition, or diagnosis and which are appropriate for the person(s).
Patient knowledge access (DC.2.7.2)	Enable the accessibility of reliable information about wellness, disease management, treatments, and related information that is relevant for a specific patient.
Support self-care (DC.2.2.1.6)	Provide the patient with decision support for self-management of a condition between patient-provider encounters.
Capture patient-originated data (DC.1.1.8)	Capture and explicitly label patient-provided and patient-entered clinical data, and support provider authentication for inclusion in patient history.
Patient access management (DC I.1.3.1)	Enable a healthcare professional to manage a patient's access to the patient's personal health information. Patient access-management includes allowing a patient access to the patient's information and restricting access by the patient or guardian to information that is potentially harmful to the patient.

* For a comprehensive and current list of HL7 EHR standard components, visit www.hl7.org/ehr.

PATIENT-PROVIDER E-COMMUNICATION: PATIENT DEMAND, PROVIDER RESISTANCE

Online Americans (90%) want to go beyond self-care and e-communicate with their physician. Over half say they are willing to change doctors or health plans to get e-access.[12] Those age 46–60 are most likely to report e-messaging with their physicians.[7] Early adopter patients who communicate online with their physicians inquire about test results (85%), prescription renewals (85%), new symptoms (73%), referral requests (72%), appointment scheduling (59%), advice on chronic conditions (49%), and administrative matters (39%).[7] Many would pay up to $10 for such access.[13]

Physicians are some of the most online Americans of all: 98% have Internet access, 87% go online at least monthly, 90% use a computer, and 43% have broadband Internet access at work.[14] These online physicians research clinical information (90%) and communicate with colleagues (63%), yet fewer than 20% communicate electronically with any of their patients, and fewer than 5% do so regularly.[15] Most physician Web sites are merely billboards, with messaging and transaction capabilities exceeding rare,[16] and only 6% of online Americans have visited their doctor's Web site.[17]

What accounts for this glaring disparity? Providers, desiring about $33 per e-encounter,[12] complain about the lack of reimbursement for e-communication[18] and fear additional unpaid work.[19] They are also concerned about liability and privacy risks.[16] Physicians reading news stories of doctors arrested, convicted, and losing licenses for prescribing for patients they have never seen, fear state legal action.[20, 21]

More fundamentally, electronic access increases patients' power relative to physicians by enhancing patient autonomy and participation in care, something many physicians find threatening.[22]

A growing body of data and experience addresses physicians' fears. Following good messaging practices[23, 24] (Table 9-2), such as reserving e-care for established patients, substantially reduces legal risks. Web messaging, unlike e-mail, offers privacy protection tools compliant with the HIPAA Privacy and Security Rules. A recent study found that e-messaging by fewer than 10% of a practice's patients was associated with an 18% decrease in telephone calls.[25] Rather than adding to clinician workload, patient e-messaging may actually increase office productivity[26] by eliminating "telephone tag," interruptions, and lost or incorrectly transcribed messages.[25, 27] A recent content analysis concluded that patients send appropriate messages and do not message excessively.[28] Recognizing these advantages, the U.S. Institute of Medicine and Department of Health and Human Services have recently advocated electronic patient-provider communication as a core functionality of an electronic health record.[27, 29]

Table 9-2: **Recommendations for Good e-Messaging Practice**[23, 24]

Appropriate purposes	• Prescription renewals • Appointment requests • Specialist referrals • Demographic and insurance information changes • Non-urgent medical issues • Monitoring chronic conditions and effects of therapy • Behavioral intervention follow-up
Inappropriate purposes	• Medical emergencies or time-sensitive issues • Issues requiring lengthy messages or long volleys of messages • Communicating bad news • Sensitive issues, if weak system security risks disclosure
Policies and procedures	• Provide e-care only to established patients • Save messages in the patient's record • Use Web messaging or encrypted e-mail rather than insecure e-mail • Route messages to appropriate personnel • Inform patients that others in the office may handle their messages • Staff, patients, and proxies must identify themselves in messages • Users must log off of their computers when leaving a computer • Hide recipient names when sending messages to multiple patients • Remind patients not to use e-communication for urgent issues • Revoke access of patients breaching policies repeatedly or egregiously • Establish and enforce message turnaround time expectations • Include the prior communication thread in message replies • Try to limit discussion to one major topic per message • Periodically verify patient e-mail addresses. • Communicate policies to staff and patients (see www.e-pcc.org)

Financial compensation is following such recognition. Group Health Cooperative of Puget Sound (GHCPS), in Washington, pays doctors $5 per patient message, up to $1,000 a year, and Kaiser Permanente Northwest (KPNW), in Oregon, pays $5 per message string. Responding to a Stanford study reporting that Web messaging patients incurred $1.92 less per month in office visit costs and $3.69 less in total health expenditures than controls,[30] health insurers are increasingly willing to reimburse for online clinical consultations.[31] The University of California Davis Health System (UCDHS) has such contracts with 80% of its nongovernmental payers, and shares the revenue with its physicians. Literature on the benefits of patient-provider e-communication is provided in Table 9-3.

Table 9-3: The Evidence-Based EHR

Selected Studies Supporting the Benefits of Electronic Patient-Provider Communication	
Patient-provider e-messaging	• 14% higher physician office productivity[26] • 18% reduction in phone volume[25] • 14% reduction in total message volume[25] • High Improved patient satisfaction[25, 26, 32] • Payer reimbursement for clinical messaging[25] • Increased provider work flexibility[25]
Online patient appointment scheduling	• Substantial reductions in telephone staff[33] • 90% reduction in patient no-show rates[33]
Uploading of data by chronic disease patients to PHRs	• Smoking cessation rates doubled[34] • Weight loss by obese patients more than doubled[35] • Glycemic control with fewer visits among Type I diabetics[36] • Improved dysfunctional thinking among depressed patients[37] • Better engagement by troubled teens with counselors[38]

E-MAIL VERSUS WEB MESSAGING

The e-communication channels currently in use between patients and physicians are e-mail, Web messaging, and transaction portals. For healthcare communications, e-mail has severe limitations. Encryption, authentication, and message routing are difficult to impossible,[39] and 84% of e-mail is spam.[40] A University of Michigan study found that e-mail may increase the communication burden on physicians and staff, and may not improve the efficiency of clinical care.[41]

Secure Web messaging, the structured, encrypted communication via Web browsers used to shop online, is an alternative to e-mail. The tools and structures available with patient-provider Web messaging offer major improvements on the weaknesses of e-mail and can generate high levels of satisfaction for all concerned.[25, 26] User ID and password authentication for patients, providers, and staff protects privacy, controls access, and prevents spam.[26] Structured forms—one for an appointment request, another for a clinical problem—can elicit the right information from patients, and allow automatic message routing, improving office efficiency.[25, 26] Encrypted credit card processing allows for medical payment and co-payments.[30]

FULL-FUNCTIONING PATIENT PORTALS

Full patient portals can combine the advantages of messaging and information lookup with interactive functionality tied to an EHR. Integrating e-access functionality with an EHR can be done by integrating a stand-alone product, such as a Web messaging system, with an existing EHR, or by purchasing or building an EHR with an embedded patient portal. Such integrated portals can capture e-message strings and prescriptions and allow patients to access their medical records. The Department of Veterans Affairs, for example, recently implemented MyHealtheVet, which lets veterans to view medical records, refill medications, look up medical information, and enter their own medical data. Others, using vendor-supplied portals[32] or homegrown portals, such as Harvard Caregroup's PatientSite,[42] offer similar functionality. Such portals are still rare, with less than 1% of online Americans having viewed their medical records online.[16] Few early adopter organizations release clinical notes to patients or allow patients to book their own appointments, although the Murray Hill Medical Group in New York, which offers a stand-alone visit scheduling system, saves $170,000 annually from reduced staff, and has reduced no-shows from 9% to 1%.[33] Implementation considerations for developing patient portals are provided in Table 9-4.

Table 9-4: Patient Portal Implementation Considerations

Review your market	• How many patients are online? • How ready are clinicians for patient e-access? • What are your competitors doing and planning?
Assess your system's readiness	• Do clinicians have computers with broadband Internet access? • Are they messaging one another? • Is senior leadership committed to patient empowerment and access?
Learn from others' experiences	• Read the literature and contact authors. • Attend conference presentations.
Review your options	• Do you have an electronic medical record with a patient connectivity module? • If not, consider a stand-alone vendor.
Propose a solution	• Develop a project plan and cost-benefit analysis. • If possible, link to other patient access initiatives. • Involve all key stakeholders, including management, compliance, and legal.
Create a project team	• Assign a project manager. • Build deployment and training teams. • Measure and report regularly to leadership, management, and clinicians.
Market to patients	• Target marketing as each site goes live. • Mass marketing after all sites and clinicians are live.

DISEASE-SPECIFIC SOLUTIONS

The e-connectivity functionality described above holds great promise for the care of patients with chronic diseases. (See Table 9-5 for other emerging trends in patient provider communication.) The University of Washington in Seattle is experimenting with having Type II diabetics upload blood sugars, review their test results and clinic notes online and communicate with their providers through secure messaging.[43] Type I diabetics at DeVos Children's Hospital in Grand Rapids, Michigan, transmit their blood sugars to a personal health record embedded in a portal. Diabetic and asthmatic patients of Partners Healthcare in Massachusetts use the internally developed site, PatientGateway, to complete online journals and review healthcare goals ahead of office visits.

Early studies of the impacts of such initiatives report encouraging results. University of California, San Diego researchers reported that smokers using a smoking cessation Web site that sent targeted e-mail messages were almost twice as likely to quit as those using a similar education-only site.[34] Obese patients enrolled in a behavioral weight loss program who received regular advice and encouragement by email lost more than twice as much weight as controls not receiving e-mails.[35] Type I diabetics at the University of Colorado who uploaded their blood sugars in lieu of an office visit achieved the same glycemic control as usual care patients, at less than half the cost.[36] Depressed patients using an interactive cognitive behavior Web site significantly improved dysfunctional thinking compared to controls who accessed an information-only site.[37] An Australian telephone and Web counseling service, "Kids Help Line," found that young people who communicated online experienced a greater sense of safety, disclosed traumatic events more quickly, and had longer and more intense counseling sessions than those who used the telephone.[38]

Table 9-5: Three-Year Prognosis

☑ Increasingly e-connected patients will receive care where and when they want.
☑ Accelerating numbers of payers will reimburse for e-care.
☑ Patients will take more educated ownership of their health by accessing a growing online library of health content.
☑ Educated patients will see their physicians more as advisors, akin to their attorneys and accountants.
☑ Interactive monitoring e-tools will allow broader application of disease management programs.
☑ Use of patient online scheduling, e-messaging and history documentation will improve provider productivity and reduce practice overhead.

Case Study 12: Message Flow Planning Key to Patient-Provider E-Messaging

Organization:	University of California, Davis Health System, Sacramento, California
Acute Care Facilities:	1
Staffed Beds:	500
Type:	Academic Medical Center

The University of California Davis Health System (UCDHS) consists of a school of medicine, trauma center, and 16 Primary Care Network (PCN) clinics in and around Sacramento, California. In early 2001, UCDHS decided to improve access to care with patient-provider e-messaging. Since building software did not support its missions of education, research, and patient care, UCDHS sought a vendor partner. UCDHS selected an application support provider (ASP), which "rents" access to its software and hardware because of their "payer pays" business model and well-designed software. By the end of 2004, 80% of UCDHS' nongovernmental payers reimbursed for clinical online visits.

Leadership buy-in was total. Ambulatory care, legal, compliance, and risk management assisted with planning a pilot in the Folsom PCN clinic. The pilot proved successful,[26] so the system was rolled out to the rest of the PCN. Each clinic created a message flow diagram in preparation for go-live, after which all clinicians and staff were trained. The clinics converged on a common message flow, with most messages filtered by medical assistants or nurses except for appointment requests (by schedulers), and referral requests (by referral coordinators). With Internet-connected computers already in place, going live required only that the ASP provider set up staff accounts and that UCDHS market to that clinic's patients.

UCDHS has since integrated this system with its EHR to consolidate workflow and is implementing the system in its faculty and resident clinics. Triage nurse filtering of all patient messages has proven a successful model for managing these clinics' intermittent clinician presence. Even prior to mass marketing, planned for when all clinics are live, over 13,000 UCDHS patients were e-messaging by the end of 2004.

Case Study 13: Physicians Manage Patient Access to Information

Organization:	Beth Israel Deaconess Medical Center, Boston, Massachusetts
Acute Care Facilities:	1
Staffed Beds:	530
Type:	Academic Medical Center
Practices:	100

The Beth Israel Deaconess Medical Center (BIDMC) is a Harvard-affiliated 530-bed hospital, with 100 owned practices and 1,200 physicians treating 750,000 patients in Boston, Massachusetts. In 1999, BIDMC decided to increase patient involvement in care by offering secure electronic, patient-centered communication. No commercial products were available, so BIDMC spent $1 million and two person-years to develop PatientSite (https://PatientSite. bidmc.harvard.edu), going live in April 2000.[42] PatientSite allows SSL-encrypted communication, provides educational resources, offers prescription renewals, appointment requests, and specialty referrals, and, through an interface to BIDMC's internally developed clinical computing system, allows patients to see their medical records. Clinician adoption is voluntary. By mid-2004, 20,000 patients and 400 clinicians and staff in 50 practices were using PatientSite. Each month, 16% of patients review their records online.

Developing PatientSite posed several challenges. First, cost: PatientSite was developed "below the radar" at a time when BIDMC was losing money. Once operational, senior management embraced PatientSite as a patient attraction and retention tool. Second, verifying identities of patients reviewing their records online was crucial. Online registration was problematic because identities could be spoofed. The solution was two-stage registration: Patients pre-register online, then are contacted by practice personnel to verify identity.

Finally, physician resistance has slowed patient enrollment. To address concerns about patients' access to their records, physicians are allowed to specify what information (laboratory, radiology, etc.) their patients can view. BIDMC is exploring how best to release clinical notes, and delays the release of results best reviewed with a clinician. BIDMC addressed fears of a heavy messaging time burden and a desire for reimbursement by showing physicians that they receive less than one message per 100 patients per day, and by developing a partnership with an ASP vendor to implement their clinical visit technology, which, per contract with several payers, triggers payment.

Case Study 14: Portal "Translates" Medical Terminology for Patients

Organization:	Group Health Cooperative of Puget Sound, Washington and Idaho
Acute Care Facilities:	2
Staffed Beds:	173
Type:	Staff Model HMO
Physicians:	1,000

Group Health Cooperative of Puget Sound is a staff model integrated care delivery system with 26 clinics, 2 hospitals, and 350,000 patients throughout

Washington and Idaho. Group Health incorporated patient e-access into its EHR through MyGroupHealth, a pre-existing Web portal. Patients can message their providers; review their lab results, visit summaries, problem list, and allergies; and request appointments and medication refills. The organizing principle for implementation was patient access to their medical records. This principle led to implementation of results-review functionality and secure messaging from the EHR as a "big bang" across the delivery system in one week.

When patients began accessing their medical records online, a key challenge was translating content from clinician to patient language. The cultural changes inherent in increasing transparency were incorporated into the EHR implementation. All clinicians understand that all data entered into the EHR, with the exception of clinician notes, is accessible by patients; inclusion of notes is being planned.

Group Health's success stems from the commitment of the entire medical group: Participation was mandatory. All 1,000 clinicians meet their patients' needs using Web services. This commitment and integration of e-health services into the EHR workflow have improved responsiveness to patients; replies to patient messages within one business day increased from 80% to 95%.

Group Health, as the first group in its area to provide a robust set of e-health services to patients, has incorporated e-health into its brand and marketing strategies. With over 65,000 patients signed up (and numbers growing rapidly), Group Health's commitment to broad connectivity with its patients allows it to differentiate itself from competitors and gain operational efficiencies.

References

1 Harris Interactive. Two in five adults keep personal or family health records and almost everybody thinks this is a good idea. *Health Care News.* 2004; 4(13).

2 Fox S. Older Americans and the Internet. Pew Internet & American Live Project 2004; March 25.

3 Holmes BJ, Bishop LF. The uninsured are not technology slouches. Forrester Research. September 3, 2003.

4 Pew Internet & America Live Project. Demographics of Internet users. May–June, 2004.

5 Fishman E. Using the "e" to save the ER. Manhattan Research 2004; October.

6 Do-it themselves diagnosis: patients pick their tests. *American Medical News.* May 5, 2003.

7 Houston TK, Sands DZ, Jenckes MW, Ford DE. Experiences of patients who were early adopters of electronic communication with their physician: satisfaction, benefits, and concerns. *Am J Managed Care.* 2004;10(9):601–608.

8 Wang M, Lau C, Matsen F, Kim Y: Personal health information management system and its application in referral management. *IEEE Trans Inf Tech Biomed.* 2004; 8(3):287–297.

9 Harris Interactive. No significant change in the number of "cyberchondriacs" – those who go online for health care information. *Health Care News.* 2004; 4(7).

10 Yasnoff WA, Humphreys BL, Overhage JM, et al. A consensus action agenda for achieving the national health information infrastructure. *J Am Med Inform Assoc.* 2004; 11(4):332–338.

11 Kandra A. Trusting your health history to the web. *PC World.* December, 2004; pp 47–50.

12 Harris Interactive. Patient/physician online communication: many patients want it, would pay for it, and it would influence their choice of doctors and health plans. *Health Care News.* 2002; 2(8).

13 Jupiter Research. Online patient-physician communication: Benchmarking consumer adoption. January 15, 2004.

14 Brown E. The next generation of wired physicians. Forrester Research. August 24, 2004.

15 Manhattan Research. Taking the Pulse 4.0: Physicians and Emerging Information Technologies. March 17, 2004.

16 Brown E. Physician websites: Not much there. Forrester Research. June 17, 2004.

17 Brown E. Why consumers visit physician group sites. Forrester Research. October 29, 2003.

18 American College of Physicians. The Changing Face of Ambulatory Medicine-Reimbursing Physicians for Computer-Based Care: ACP Analysis and Recommendations to Assure Fair Reimbursement for Physician Care Rendered Online (Policy Paper). Philadelphia: American College of Physicians; 2003.

19 Sands DZ. Help for physicians contemplating use of e-mail with patients. *J Am Med Inform Assoc.* 2004; 11:268–269.

20 Chin T. Firm treating strangers by web shut out by Illinois directive. *American Medical News.* November 4, 2002.

21 Stewart P. Legal trends in e-health care. *Group Practice Journal.* February, 2002; pp 11–17.

22 Winkelman WJ, Leonard KJ. Overcoming structural constraints to patient utilization of electronic medical records: a critical review and proposal for an evaluation framework. *J Am Med Inform Assoc.* 2004; 11(2):151–161.

23 Kane B, Sands DZ, for the AMIA Internet Working Group, Task Force on Guidelines for the Use of Clinic-Patient Electronic Mail. Guidelines for the clinical use of electronic mail with patients. *J Am Med Inform Assoc.* 1998; 5:104–111.

24 Sands DZ. Guidelines for the use of patient-centered electronic mail. Chapter in: *Leading the Way to Information Exchange in the Electronic World*; Massachusetts Health Data Consortium; April 1999; pp 28–40.

25 Liederman EM, Lee JC, Baquero VH, Seites PG. Patient-physician Web messaging: The impact on message volume and satisfaction. *J Gen Intern Med.* 2005; 20(1):52

26 Liederman EM, Morefield CS. Web messaging: a new tool for patient-physician communication. *J Am Med Inform Assoc.* 2003; 10:263–274.

27 Institute of Medicine. *Key Capabilities of an Electronic Health Record.* Washington, D.C.:National Academies Press; 2003; pp 9–17.

28 White CB, Moyer CA, Stern DT, et al. A content analysis of e-mail communication between patients and their providers: patients get the message. *J Am Med Inform Assoc.* 2004; 11(4): 260–267.

29 U.S. Department of Health and Human Services. A decade of health information technology: delivering consumer-centric and information-rich health care. 2004; July 21.

30 Baker L. The RelayHealth webVisit Study: Final Report. 2003; January.

31 Kowalczyk L. Insurers to pay physicians to answer questions over web. *Boston Globe.* May 24, 2004.

32 Hassol A, Walker JM, Kidder D, et al. Patient experiences and attitudes about access to a patient electronic health care record and linked web messaging. *J Am Med Inform Assoc.* 2004; 11(6):505–513.

33 Versel N. Online reservations: letting patients make their own appointments. *American Medical News.* March, 2004; p 22.

34 Lenert L, Munoz RF, Perez JE, Bansod A. Automated e-mail messaging as a tool for improving quit rates in an Internet smoking cessation intervention. *J Am Med Inform Assoc.* 2004; 11:235–240.

35 Tate DF, Wing RR, Winett RA. Using Internet technology to deliver a behavioral weight loss program. *JAMA.* 2001; 285(9):1172–1177.

36 Chase HP, Roberts MD, Pearson JA, et al. Modem transmission of glucose values reduces the costs and need for clinic visits. *Diab Care.* 2003; 26(5):1475–1479.

37 Christensen H, Griffiths KM, Jorm AF. Delivering interventions for depression by using the Internet: randomised controlled trial. *BMJ.* 2004; 328(7434):265.

38 Wootton R, Yellowlees P, McLaren P. *Telepsychiatry and E-mental Health*. London: Royal Society of Medicine Press; 2003.

39 First Consulting Group. Online patient-provider communication tools. *iHealth Reports*. California Healthcare Foundation. November, 2003.

40 MessageLabs. Olympus America Uses MessageLabs to Combat Spam, Viruses and Other Unwanted Email Threats. Press Release 2004; September 14. Available at http://www.messagelabs.com/news/pressreleases/detail/default.asp?contentItemId=1141&region=.

41 Katz SJ, Moyer CA, Cox DT, et al. Effect of a triage-based e-mail system on clinic resource use and patient and physician satisfaction in primary care. *J Gen Intern Med*. 2003; 18:736–44.

42 Sands DZ, Halamka JD. PatientSite: Patient centered communication, services, and access to information. Chapter in: Nelson R, Ball MJ. *Consumer Informatics: Applications and Strategies in Cyber Health Care*. New York: Springer-Verlag; 2004.

43 Ralston JD, Revere D, Robins LS, Golberg HI. Patients' experience with a diabetes support programme based on an interactive electronic medical record: qualitative study. *BMJ*. 2004; 328:1159–1162.

CHAPTER 10

Data Sharing and Interoperability

Edward Ewen, MD, FACP

In addition to being reliable, timely, and accurate, healthcare information today must also be portable. Portability is required to deliver effective patient care across the vast array of healthcare providers spanning a wide variety of clinical settings. Caregivers and their patients expect that clinical information should be sharable, whether between applications, hospitals, or care settings. The options for organizations seeking to improve the portability of information are enormous but often not easy to execute. This chapter addresses the important issues of how information can be shared, the standards that are in place to support data sharing, and considerations for selecting an approach.

THE CASE FOR HEALTH INFORMATION SHARING

Healthcare today is provided by a dynamic and increasingly complex array of caregivers. While receiving care a patient frequently encounters a host of providers, including primary care physicians, hospitalists, specialists, ancillary providers, pharmacies, hospitals, laboratories, and imaging centers. The rise of consumerism, rapid advances in medical technology requiring greater specialization, and reimbursement limitations driving physicians to further narrow the scope of their practices all but guarantee this trend will continue. To further complicate matters, the majority of these caregivers function within their own information silos. Even though patients may move from place to place in the healthcare landscape, their information frequently does not move with them.

This wide distribution of healthcare responsibilities across numerous and changing panels of providers without the parallel distribution of critical healthcare information

Deborah Kohn, RHIA, CHE, CPHIMS, contributed the sections on regional health information organizations and the national health information network, and Case Study 15 on Internet-Derived Technologies Contribute to RHIO's Success.

lays the groundwork for our error-prone and inefficient healthcare delivery system. Our tools are created to support specific clinical processes usually occurring within a single organization. For a clinician caring for a patient longitudinally or across healthcare settings, this application-centric view is largely irrelevant, often distracting, and sometimes dangerous.

Sharing data across multiple settings should result in significant clinical and economic benefits. The majority of these benefits flow from one fundamental assumption: clinician access to more complete and timely information will result in better decision making. Better decision-making yields better clinical outcomes and improved efficiency. The improvements in efficiency will largely result from reductions in duplicate testing, administrative overhead, and medical errors that complicate care and drive increased costs.

BARRIERS TO INFORMATION SHARING

There are at least three significant types of barriers to information sharing in healthcare today. These types relate to organizational issues, cost and complexity, and standards.

- *Organizational:* Sharing data within an organization requires considerable trust and commitment between contributing parties. An appreciation for cultural differences, an understanding of disparate vocabularies, and open lines of communication are important success factors. This is an even greater issue when sharing data across organizational boundaries.
- *Cost and Complexity:* Building bridges between data sources can be a complex and resource-intensive task. The underlying complexity may also make it difficult to firmly establish scope and define requirements and contributes further to cost.
- *Data Standards:* The lack of established or consistently used data standards provides a significant barrier to data sharing. The need to turn to proprietary or internally developed solutions complicates implementation and interoperability while driving cost even higher.

This chapter focuses primarily on the issues related to data standards.

MAJOR OPPORTUNITIES

The opportunities to share data and the approach taken by a specific organization will vary depending on circumstances. Table 10-1 illustrates two organizational extremes and the different challenges faced by organizations under these circumstances. The examples describe individual organizations; however, the basic issues apply when sharing data externally as well.

DATA STANDARDS

Data standards related to person/patient identification, communication, data definition, and security are central issues common to all data-sharing efforts. The challenge of sharing healthcare data is not simply one of identifying and merging data from across disparate system domains. Healthcare data is separated not just geographically, but also by disparate conceptualization, structure, and codification. In order to successfully combine data into a clinically coherent presentation, we must be able to receive and interpret that data, assign it to the correct persons, and place it in the appropriate knowledge context. This requires interoperability standards (Table 10-2) in key areas: person identification, communication, and codification.

Table 10-1: Provider Data-Sharing Challenges

Example	Circumstances	Challenge
Multiple, formerly separate, hospitals under one parent organization with a variety of redundant administrative and clinical systems	• Horizontal integration • Similar functionality • Narrow clinical context • High redundancy	• Data standards often exist, but may not be applied consistently across duplicate systems • Little need to modify data format and presentation • Example: sharing lab data across hospitals may require standardization using LOINC
Primary care practices, hospitals, home care, and health insurance plans organized along a continuum of care	• Vertical integration • Disparate functions • Wide clinical context • Less redundancy	• Data standards may not exist for sharing across healthcare contexts • Data presentation needs vary considerably depending on clinical context • Example: no standard exists to facilitate sharing allergy data between office and hospital settings

Table 10-2: Interoperability Standards

Data Standard	Description	Examples*
Person identification	Associates data with the patient or provider	Unique identifier, MPI
Communication	Defines structure and delivery of data	HL7, DICOM, NCPDP
Codification	Allows data to be merged, combined, manipulated, and re-used	ICD9, CPT, LOINC, SNOMED, NDC
Security	Addresses privacy and accountability	SSL, HL7v3

* HL7 - Health Level Seven; DICOM - Digital Imaging and Communications in Medicine; NCPDP - National Council of Prescription Drug Programs; ICD -International Classifications of Disease; CPT - Current Procedural Terminology; LOINC - Logical Observation Identifiers, Names and Codes; SNOMED - Systematic Nomenclature of Medicine; NDC - National Drug Codes; SSL - Secure Sockets Layer.

Integrating the Healthcare Enterprise (IHE), a cooperative initiative between healthcare providers and industry, is leading efforts to coordinate the application of existing standards to improve patient care through greater interoperability and data sharing. The IHE has assembled implementation profiles that do not replace existing standards, but rather provide definition on the proper implementation of these standards. These profiles are intended to organize discussion around integration needs. Industry may use them to guide future product development. Healthcare organizations may find they facilitate vendor selection and contracting by providing a framework for comparing standards implementations and better estimating integration costs.

PERSON/PATIENT IDENTIFICATION

Much of the data collected in healthcare is attached to a specific context or process, such as an acute care admission or ambulatory visit. However, the single common thread across all systems and settings is the patient. If we can identify the patient, positively and uniquely, then we can begin to share and re-use his or her health information.

There are two primary approaches to patient identification in use today: the single unique identifier and the master patient index (MPI). Each method must balance the need to identify patients with privacy concerns and practical implementation issues. The weight given to each of these concerns will vary depending on the context of data sharing.

A single unique identifier is a key that identifies individuals across information systems. This approach can result in a simple, efficient, and accurate means of linking records across systems. Though the solution in concept is relatively simple, there are some complex issues related to the generation, management, and storage of a unique identifier that can make this difficult to implement outside the scope of a single organization. The resulting ease in matching records to specific patients also leads to this method's greatest drawback: the relative ease by which privacy may be violated. At the present time there is no nationally recognized unique patient identifier, and the HIPAA regulations requiring such an identifier have been put on hold indefinitely. An alternative is a Voluntary Patient Identifier. This would provide a single patient identifier but allow citizens to "opt-in" to the program instead of making it mandatory, thus addressing some of the concerns of privacy advocates regarding a national identifier.

An MPI attempts to assign identity based on demographic data submitted by the various systems without the use of a universal identifier. An index is then created linking the various system identifiers to the descriptive and demographic information provided by the patient. Matching algorithms are used to create and maintain the index. Sometimes referred to as a "federated" approach, this concept was backed by Connecting for Health. This approach is inherently less accurate in terms of identification because of the probabilistic nature of the matching algorithms. Human intervention is often needed to adjudicate the inevitable discrepancies, duplications, and misassignments. The approach also has also generated privacy concerns as it requires the sharing of a patient's personal information (e.g., name, age, gender) every time there is a need to link a patient's information.

COMMUNICATION

Communication or message standards relate to the structure and delivery of data. Health Level Seven (HL7) is the most widely applied messaging standard in healthcare and is principally concerned with clinical and administrative data. DICOM is another important messaging standard used to transmit radiologic images. The Continuity of Care Record (CCR) is a relatively new, XML-based messaging standard designed to transmit key health information as a patient transitions from one healthcare context to another. These transitions would include, for example, the referral of a patient from a primary care physician to a specialist, or the discharge of a patient from the hospital to home care.

CODIFICATION

Successfully transmitting and then linking data to a specific patient is only the initial step in a relatively limited form of data sharing. Data sharing becomes most useful when there is a clear and shared understanding of the meaning behind the data. This is achievable only through the use of shared, unambiguous, controlled vocabularies. These vocabularies standardize and codify the information content, allowing receiving systems to correctly interpret and represent this data in the shared context. These code standards allow the data to maintain fidelity during transfer, ensuring that the data arrives with no more or no less meaning than the originating system intended. Some common examples of controlled vocabularies include the ICD-9, CPT, SNOMED, NDC, and LOINC.

Codification is essential for sophisticated reuse of information, such as the use of allergy data from one system in the drug-drug interaction checking utility of a pharmacy system. Some specific types of information to be shared and some of the challenges encountered are listed in Table 10-3.

Table 10-3: Communication and Coding Standards for Select EHR Data

Information	Communication	Coding
Allergies	HL7	No standard
Medications	NCPDP, HL7	NDC (primarily designed for inventory management)
Problem/procedure list	HL7	ICD, CPT, SNOMED …
Transfer summary	CCR	Uses any available coding standard
Narrative reports	HL7	No standard
Radiology images	DICOM	DICOM, CPT, ICD

OPPORTUNITIES FOR SHARING DATA INTERNALLY

The primary advantage to sharing data internally rather than externally is in the ability of an organization to establish and enforce standards that promote data sharing. Challenges that persist in this setting include the tendency for data to be oriented to a single episode or process of care, the possibility that electronic data may be periodically purged from operational systems, and the multiplicity of identifiers native to each system that must either be reconciled or synchronized with each other.

OVERVIEW OF STRATEGIES

Faced with a variety of clinical applications and the need to share or exchange data between them, organizations generally have taken one or more of five basic strategies. Organizations will often use a combination of all five of these strategies. The strategy selected impacts on functionality and implementation effort. Table 10-4 suggests what functional capabilities exist for these approaches.

A. Baseline: No Data Sharing

Individual software applications are made available; however, no effort is made to share data between these applications. The clinician must search for information by signing on to each system, search for the patient using demographic data, and collecting and consolidating this information either by writing it down or printing out data sets for later use. This approach is inefficient, prone to errors, and discourages clinician use of information systems. Patient identification is handled by the clinician as he or she manually searches for the patient in each system. Messaging is not used and vocabulary standards are handled at the application level. A common minor adjustment to this approach simply makes the application's icons available on a standard web page or portal. This saves the practitioner some time searching for applications, however, involves no data sharing even in terms of person identification.

Table 10-4: Internal Data-Sharing Models

	A. Stand Alone Applications	B. Information Portal	C. Brokered Peer- to-Peer	D. Interfaced Applications	E. Integrated Application Suite
Data elements shared	None	Identifiers	Identifiers Clinical data	Identifiers Clinical data	Identifiers Clinical data
Data imported/ exported	No	No	No	Yes	Not Necessary
Single data model	No	No	No	No	Yes
Standards required					+
Person identification	No	Yes	Yes	Yes	Yes
Communication	No	Yes	Yes	Yes	Yes
Codification	No	No	No	Yes	Yes
Enhanced functionality					+
Improved access	No	Yes	Yes	No	Yes
Flexible data Presentation	No	No	Yes	Application specific	Application specific
Merged data elements	No	No	No	Yes	Yes
Automated decision support	No	No	No	Yes	Yes

Less ← Data Sharing → More

B. Clinical Information Portal

In this strategy, data sharing occurs at the level of the user interface, most often through the use of a Web-based portal. This model provides more efficient access to systems by sharing provider and patient identifying data. Using single sign-on and/or clinical context management (CCOW), clinicians are able to sign in once and open selected clinical systems without repeating the sign-on procedure. Context management allows the user to maintain the patient context when navigating between applications, allowing clinicians to avoid repeatedly searching for a patient as they navigate from, for example, an ambulatory EHR to a hospital imaging system. This strategy allows an organization to avoid the difficult task of actually importing or exporting clinical data while delivering some of the usability benefits of information sharing to the clinician at the point of care. It is a relatively less complex implementation that requires an organization to standardize user and patient identification, but not necessarily data definitions. A significant limitation of this approach is the inability to re-use information for automated decision support. Since the information is not coded or brought internal to the application, the data cannot be used to support processing within that application.

C. Brokered Peer-to-Peer Networks

Some clinical information portals will actually go a step further and extract a limited set of information from contributing systems and present it through a Web interface. In this model a central index matches personal identifiers with the addresses or pointers to data elements in the originating system. When data is created in the source system it notifies the index of the identity of the patient and the address of the information. When a user requests information, the index looks up the associated pointers and queries the contributing systems. The systems then return the actual data and it is temporarily assembled and presented to the user. This strategy is, in effect, a peer-to-peer network "brokered" by a master patient-pointer index. The clinical data remains in the originating systems and is only virtually combined at the level of the user interface. This approach requires careful attention to personal identifiers and messaging standards, but does not require standard codification. This approach allows an organization to share data from a potentially wide array of disparate legacy systems and present it in a flexible format through a single sign-on and patient search. The investment in existing systems can be leveraged, and some of the work standardizing data definitions can be avoided. Because the actual data, however, is not imported into these various source systems, automated decision support using shared data elements is impossible.

D. System Interfacing

This approach carries data sharing beyond the user interface and into the actual software systems. Identification, messaging, and codification standards are employed to bring data across an interface directly into the receiving application. Once internalized, this information can be used to support any of the functionality, including automated decision support, inherent in the receiving system. This strategy supports the greater functionality and flexibility, but requires close attention to data standards. It also results in significant interdependencies between systems, complicating systems upgrades and downtime procedures.

E. System Integration

This strategy attempts to provide wide-ranging clinical functionality though a single application suite, presumably using a single data model to facilitate information exchange between components. The practical implementation of this strategy centers on installing large, complex, single vendor application sets. In theory these applications share data internally by using a single universal data model. Unfortunately, many of these "integrated" products today contain legacy data structures resulting in a variety of internal data models. The data sharing that results is, in effect, a form of internal interfacing, and is most similar to the system interfacing strategy.

OPPORTUNITIES FOR SHARING DATA EXTERNALLY

Two important recent developments are likely to impact significantly on external data sharing: the growing interest in regional and national health information infrastructures (RHII, NHII) and the development of the CCR standard (see Chapter 4).

National Health Information Network

The NHIN (formerly National Health Information Infrastructure or NHII) is a government sponsored initiative designed to improve the effectiveness, efficiency and overall quality of health and healthcare in the U.S. This will be accomplished by providing a comprehensive view of a patient's health information at the point of care through the development of a comprehensive, interconnected, knowledge-based network of interoperable systems from all sectors of the healthcare industry. Also referred to as the "Medical Internet," providers of care will be able to electronically exchange the information between all electronic health records so that a complete, electronic health record can be assembled whenever and wherever a patient presents for care.

The Department of Health and Human Services has provided the initial guiding principles and requirements for this network. The NHIN will be built incrementally from collaborative local and regional efforts in the public and private sector. Activities on the national level will most likely focus on the development and/or adoption of standards and economic incentives that will promote the growth of these regional infrastructures.

The NHIN was mentioned first by the Institute of Medicine (IOM) in their seminal report, *The Computer-based Patient Record: An Essential Technology for Health Care.*[1] The NHIN was defined further by the National Committee on Vital and Health Statistics (NCVHS) in their report, *Information for Health: A Strategy for Building the NHII.*[2] The NHIN gained national attention by both public and private sectors following September 11, 2001, and the anthrax attacks, when the need for enhanced public health surveillance and response became more visible and immediate.

Obstacles to NHIN include the current lack of standards allowing for interoperability and data sharing, insufficient funding, the lack of ongoing economic incentives needed to sustain infrastructure operations, and public concern over privacy.

The data-sharing strategies available to support an NHIN are fundamentally no different from those available to individual organizations. In this case, however, the decision on the approach used must carefully weigh public concerns over privacy and organizational concerns over the continued ownership, control, and advantage their data provides them. As a result, today's NHIN focus is to begin with a network of connected, public and private Regional Health Information Organizations (RHIOs; formerly Local Health Information Infrastructures or LHIIs), each facilitating exchange of health information in a "region."

Regional Health Information Organizations (RHIOs)

RHIOs are healthcare provider, payor, and patient collaboratives that serve anywhere from approximately 500,000 – 1,000,000+ lives. Typically, a RHIO is made up of diverse healthcare stakeholders providing and receiving services in a medical referral area or area served by a regional Emergency Medical Services organization. As such, RHIOs are bigger and fewer than the earlier LHIIs. However, typically, RHIOs are no larger than a state (Oregon, Wyoming, Illinois, Delaware).

Many developing RHIOs favor a decentralized or "federated" approach to their technical architectures, similar to the brokered peer-to-peer model described above. This model is NOT the fully integrated, monolithic, centralized database model.

Instead, this model consists of distinct, distributed, disparate, decentralized databases (also known as the 5Ds). Centralization ONLY occurs with an Enterprise-type Master Patient Index (EMPI, also known as Identity Management) for demographic data, and, perhaps, with Application Programming Interfaces (APIs). As such, this model allows information sharing to occur without requiring a national patient identifier and allows contributing organizations to retain ownership and control of their data.

The federated model has other advantages. For example, data ownership is managed by defining business policies and access rules. In addition, typically, new computer systems are not required, allowing for an easier transition to regional electronic health records.

Unfortunately, the drawbacks of this approach remain. Since there is no unified data model and standardized codification, decision support and many reporting capabilities are limited. In addition, typically, this approach requires more coordination to implement. For example, often RHIO stakeholders have to accept diverse, regional infrastructures and workflows.

Case Study 15: Internet-Derived Technologies Contribute to RHIO's Success

Organization:	Taconic Health Information Network and Community (THINC), Fishkill, New York
Physicians:	2,500
Covered Lives:	2,000,000 in six Hudson Valley NY counties
Type:	Federated, with Inconsistent Databases

In 2004, the Agency for Healthcare Research and Quality (AHRQ) awarded the Taconic Health Information Network and Community (THINC) a $1.5M patient safety grant to assist them in adding a healthcare portal and other Internet-derived technologies, such as web services and peer-to-peer networking, to its existing, community-wide electronic data exchange system. In addition, the grant will assist THINC in incorporating an electronic medical record (EMR) system into this technology infrastructure. As such, the not-for-profit Taconic Independent Physician Association (IPA) will be one of the nation's first physician organizations to deploy a standard EMR within a RHIO. Similar systems exist in large, integrated delivery networks and developing RHIOs, but few exist in community settings with independently practicing physicians.

For three years Taconic worked to develop the cooperation needed among its multiple, diverse, and often competing stakeholders—physicians, acute care hospitals, reference laboratories and insurers—to succeed with health information exchange. This was accomplished by implementing its data exchange system. In this system, all network addressable devices (e.g., desktop, laptop, and PDA-type computers) act as clients to a centralized server that securely stores and forwards any type of digital file from the stakeholders' systems—audio, coded, image, text, or video data file, such as laboratory results. This allows authenticated and authorized users on the network to retrieve those files via online pull or offline push, when required.

The Web portal additionally permits the physician members of the Taconic IPA to access electronic health data, treatment protocols, and clinical research and to share clinical information throughout the region. For example, the RHIO's stakeholders sign-on to multiple data sources with a single password and user ID, search the diverse, multiple stakeholder systems for information, such as diagnoses, tests, procedures, patient names, etc., and easily access RHIO health partner organizations' multiple sources of structured and unstructured data. In addition, the Taconic IPA physicians individually customize the portal's look-and-feel based on each physician's unique role and preferences, such as links to sports channels or patient lists. The Web portal leverages the physician's previous habits and known, observed and predictive profile information by making automatic decisions about what data to display and how to display it and creates taxonomies or categories to classify the physician's files and data by, for example, test results, dictations, and patients.

By spring 2005, the EMR will allow Taconic physicians to electronically send prescriptions to pharmacists. The e-prescribing capabilities of the EMR will check for interactions with other drugs a patient is taking, suggest a dosage, and inform the patient what the co-payment for that drug is likely to be.

Members of the Taconic IPA have no-cost access to the basic portal and EMR functions, such as the search and e-prescribing capabilities. Additional portal and EMR capabilities requires a monthly $500 fee, which is not covered by THINC.

References

1 *The Computer-based Patient Record: An Essential Technology for Health Care.* Institute of Medicine; 1991.

2 *Information for Health: A Strategy for Building the NHII.* National Committee on Vital and Health Statistics; 2001.

SECTION IV

IMPLEMENTATION CONSIDERATIONS

CHAPTER 11

Implementing the Ambulatory EHR

Laura Jantos, MBA, MHA, FHIMSS

Ambulatory EHR systems, while less complex than their acute care counterparts, are nonetheless challenging to implement. Most ambulatory practices have limited IT resources, minimal experience with major system implementations, and complicated processes and workflows. While EHRs offer significant benefits, a problematic implementation is likely to wreak organizational and financial havoc on the typical practice. This chapter addresses some of the unique challenges that confront the physician practice, small or large, once the EHR product has been selected and the organization is ready to automate the clinical practice. Chapter 3 focuses on the earlier stage of EHR planning for the ambulatory practice.

Unfortunately, implementing an ambulatory EHR is not as easy as installing the latest version of shrink-wrapped software. The question as to why EHR implementation is not easy is the subject of national interest and debate, but this chapter focuses on a few key issues that are pertinent to practices of any size and can make a significant impact on the success of the implementation. While there are many successful models for implementing an EHR in a group setting, it is imperative that each group evaluate the benefits they hope to achieve through use of this new technology and manage their implementation to ensure that these benefits are realized. This chapter discusses how to customize and manage an implementation to meet organizational objectives and ensure the likelihood of success.

Robert J. Lamberts, MD, contributed Case Study 16 on Eight-Year-Old EHR Continues to Evolve. David Kane, CPA, MBA, contributed Case Study 17 on Practice Realizes Quick Physician Adoption.

A PAINLESS ROLLOUT

Unlike practice management or other types of systems, ambulatory EHRs are almost never implemented in a "big bang" fashion, but rather are phased in, both in terms of functionality and users. Maximum benefit from an ambulatory EHR is obtained once all providers are using the system at the point of care. However, getting to this point can require significant time and resources. To ease the transition, both system functionality and users are phased-in over a period of time. When deciding how to phase in functionality, consider beginning with "easy" functions (such as reviewing results) and incorporating more complex functions, such as encounter documentation, in the first few weeks of the go-live. Integrating data from other systems, such as transcription or laboratory, can provide a base of information that makes the system useful from the start. Because integrating data into a new system can also be a complex task, many organizations identify a point of time and move forward with interfaced information as it is created rather than trying to load an extensive history of information.

It may also be advantageous to abstract important information from paper records to the EHR prior to seeing the patient for the first time on the EHR. This information might include problem list, allergies and immunizations, and social and family history.

The advantage of abstracting information is that it is available as a data point in the record and can be searched. It can also be used to satisfy health maintenance reminders and alerts, so that when the system is used for the first time, these "bells and whistles" can be implemented without interrupting providers too much.

Data that is typically entered once the system is live includes current medications and prescriptions, encounter notes, orders, referrals, and so forth.

Given the effort and cost associated with scanning and abstracting strategies, many organizations have reduced or sharply discontinued these practices in favor of asking the provider to see the patient with the paper chart, abstracting key data during or after the first EHR-based visit, and then flagging any important pieces of information to be scanned post-visit. After a few EHR-based visits, the paper chart can usually be archived.

It is important to have a strategy on an ongoing basis to manage paper that is received, such as discharge summaries, external lab results, and specialty consults. These may be scanned or abstracted. Table 11-1 provides examples of documentation that may be scanned instead of abstracted. Check with state law regarding records retention to ensure that a particular document strategy is compliant.

Table 11-1: Data Entry Methods

Scanned (Typically Not Searchable)	Abstracted (Searchable Data Points)	Validated/Re-entered
• Treatment plan • Discharge summary • Advance directives	• Allergies • Immunization history • Family/social history • Surgical history	• Problem list • Medication list

DOCUMENTATION TOOLS

Encounter documentation tools are the forms, drop-down lists, predesigned visit notes, and other shortcuts that enable providers to document a patient visit. For example, an online form could be created for a patient physical that would include a review of systems, common diagnoses, typical procedures, medications, orders, referrals, and E&M coding. Most EHR systems come with a basic set of customizable encounter documentation templates. Although tools for customization vary, they may include macros, trees, phrases, shortcuts, and synonyms. The degree to which templates can be customized by individual providers varies by system and by organization. In any case, either developing or reviewing and adopting available encounter documentation tools is a time-consuming but important part of configuring an EHR.

A smaller practice will typically allow each provider to develop and maintain their own templates. In a larger practice, especially one with many specialties and locations, development and maintenance of templates may require dedicated staff. In a large implementation, the ability to develop effective templates and train physicians regarding their use is a significant factor in determining how quickly the organization can deploy the EHR.

PROVIDER PHASING

Many EHR implementations fail because the enthusiasm of the physician who is most interested in the system is not shared by his or her colleagues. Therefore, when considering how to phase in users, it is important not only to select someone who is computer-literate, but who will also be objective and capable of identifying areas needing enhancement prior to being used by other providers. After this initial trial (which may include more than one provider, and may be focused on a specific location, team, or specialty), subsequent groups may be identified based on priorities and/or benefit to the group, such as.

- **Ease of Implementation:** Starting with the most accepting providers and then proceeding onto those who challenge the concept of the EHR will provide opportunity to sway people who are reluctant.
- **Related Entities:** Grouping providers or specialties that work together into a functional sequence can help reduce paperwork and headaches. An example would be ensuring that orthopedics and physical therapy are implemented simultaneously.
- **Facilities or Workflow Implications:** Evaluating need to revise workspaces, or workflows, to be more efficient with the EHR.

Once the EHR has interfaced data, access can be given to a wide group to view results (lab, transcription) until training in more sophisticated functions can be provided.

STAFFING REQUIREMENTS: IDENTIFYING APPROPRIATE RESOURCES AND REQUIREMENTS

Finding appropriate resources to manage an implementation and then support the EHR once it has been implemented can be challenging, especially for practices without dedicated information systems resources.

Vendors typically provide resources to train some or all clinic staff in how to use the application and to guide the system setup process. They may provide a project manager (PM), whose job is to ensure that the project is completed in a timely manner and to coordinate among the vendor's implementation team, which can include trainers, implementers, and technical resources. Depending on size, the practice is typically expected to provide its own PM, application specialists, and (for larger organizations) trainers. These resources are in addition to informal project team resources such as physician advocates, nursing advocates, and individuals responsible for scanning and/ or abstracting information from paper charts into the EHR.

Key project roles for the clinic include:

- **Project Manager:** The PM is responsible for ensuring that day-to-day project tasks are completed by clinic implementation team members and for holding the vendor's PM accountable.
- **Project Owner (PO):** The PO is typically a physician, and is the person who is the chief advocate for use of the EHR.
- **Project Staff:** The number and type of project staff needed for an EHR implementation varies greatly depending on the size of the organization and the complexity of the system being implemented. The role of the project staff is to configure the system, develop interfaces or imports, perform testing, develop procedural documentation, train end users, and support the go-live.

It may be advantageous to train individuals from within the organization to fill new project roles. If this is not possible, the organization may need to look outside to identify third-party organizations (such as consulting firms) that can assist in the implementation. This may be the case if: (1) internal staff cannot be diverted from their day-to-day duties to assist in the implementation to the extent necessary to be successful; and (2) internal staff are not skilled in managing large projects or lack the skills necessary to understand the project plan, especially tasks that the vendor may not have documented as part of its standard implementation plan but which are critical (e.g., procurement of hardware from a third party or development of the practice management system side of the interfaces).

Table 11-2 provides an overview of these individuals, as well as others, and their relative levels of effort for a moderate-size practice implementation.

PROJECT ORGANIZATIONAL STRUCTURE

Key components of the project team may include (depending on the size of the organization):

- *Project Steering Committee:* The role of the steering committee is to provide oversight and input into major project decisions. The committee typically consists of practice administration, key physicians, IT leadership, and the PM.
- *Project Manager or Project Management Office (PMO):* In a larger organization, a PMO may be created to ensure that the various organizational initiatives (both IT-related and non-IT-related) are controlled in a consistent manner, and that implications among projects are well understood.

• **Work Groups:** The project may need a group of individuals to complete key project tasks, such as configuring the system (loading data into tables and pull-down menus).

The project team composition may be different than the system selection process.

Table 11-2: Staffing for a Medium to Large Ambulatory Implementation

Person (# of FTEs)	Level of Effort (Percentage of FTE)		
	Planning	Configuration and Testing	Training and Rollout
Project manager (1)	100%	100%	100%
Physician advocate (1)	25% to 75%	25%	75%
Clinical coordinator (1)	25% to 75%	25%	75%
Health information management manager	75%	75%	25%
Scanners/abstractors (TBD)	–	25%	100%
Site/area leaders	10%	10%	50% to 75%
Administrator	25% to 50%	25%	25% to 50%
Training staff (TBD)	25%	25%	100%
Information services (TBD)	25% to 100%	50% to 100%	100%
Other project staff	10% to 50%	10% to 50%	50% to 75%

DEVELOPING A DETAILED IMPLEMENTATION PLAN

A vendor's standard implementation plan is based on an "average" client. Since all practices have different characteristics and priorities, it is important to understand the assumptions that have been used in creating the standard plan and make appropriate adjustments. An overview of the typical implementation phases, activities, and durations is provided in Table 11-3.

INCORPORATING WORKFLOW REDESIGN

Workflow redesign is important because evaluating workflows enables an organization to determine how they can best use the EHR, rather than simply automating paper-based processes. To analyze work flows, many organizations perform a baseline assessment to understand pre-EHR staffing and organizational structure, cost, benchmark statistics, and processes. From this, they develop a future vision for operations that includes refined processes and staffing as well as other targets.

Statistics gathered prior to and after the implementation can identify the impact of the EHR. These include:
• Number and FTEs of providers and support staff, by type;
• Annual visit volumes by provider;
• Charge lag (in days);
• Encounters without charges (rolling average); and
• Transcription and medical records costs.

Table 11-3: Implementation Phases

Phase	Key Activities	Duration
Planning	• Appoint project team members • Determine rollout sequence • Finalize data conversion and interfaces • Train people responsible for configuring the system • Establish a baseline of current operations (statistical and process)	1–3 Months
Configuration	• Set up system files and "look-and-feel" of configurable screens • Design future desired workflows and staffing (including IT support) • Develop encounter documentation tools for key visit types, procedures, and the like. • Convert existing data • Develop interfaces	3–6 Months
Testing	Test the system and processes, as follows: • Unit test – each component by itself (drop-down menus, files, interfaces, converted data) • Integrated test – full workflows (front-to-back) including all interfaces • Stress test – volumes approximating normal daily use • Parallel test – validate data from the system against manual operations (e.g., encounter forms, medical records, etc.)	1 Month
Training	• Train end-users in use of the system as well as revised procedures • Provide generic PC training as well as system training	1 Month
Go-live/rollout	• Create a "production" system environment (while keeping a "testing" or "training" copy of the system) • Start loading data into the system for live use (scanning and/or abstracting) • Begin using the system with initial providers or at a single site • Resolve any post-live system and/or process issues • Continue rollout to subsequent providers and locations	3 Months to Years

Additional criteria may be gathered depending on the type and complexity of the practice, such as the time spent in administrative duties by clinical personnel, information systems-related costs, and turnaround on in-house tests and transcription.

Documenting key processes allows the practice to understand important handoffs and interdependencies and also provides a snapshot of potential opportunities, such as redundancies, gaps, or overlaps. Sample work flows may include:
• Patient check-in and rooming;
• Vitals and pre-provider process;
• Provider encounter (documentation, orders, prescriptions);
• In-house procedures and referrals;
• Check-out and referrals to external entities; and
• Telephone encounters.

If the clinic or group is complex, it is important to document the variability in processes among different locations, pods, or specialties. At a minimum, the organization should note variations peculiar to individual sites or referral patterns. The organization may also want to denote differences in processes for new versus established patients. Documentation should provide a model for the organization and indicate any areas where computer systems are currently in use. Some EHR products may even be able to modify their screen flow to accommodate different workflow scenarios.

In reviewing flows and statistics, some immediate enhancements (pre-EHR) may be identified. Others, however, will require some design and testing in conjunction with the implementation of the EHR, and typically some refinement prior to and following live operations. Remember that implementing an EHR is an evolving process that requires time to learn how to use the system, and that both the system and processes may change as users become more familiar with each.

SYSTEM TESTING AND ACCEPTANCE

The system should be thoroughly tested prior to live use in order to minimize any disruptions once the system is used in a clinical setting. The purpose of testing is to validate both the system and related processes. This includes ensuring that all configuration decisions made during the implementation process have been entered into the system correctly and that the system responds in a timely manner.

To support testing, most products include (or organizations negotiate) either a "testing" or a "training" environment, which is an area that is usually a replica of the "production" or "live" version of the software. In a large practice environment, it may be advantageous to have three distinct environments. An individual should be appointed to manage the environments so that modifications made in the testing environment are copied or entered into the production environment in a controlled fashion once they have been tested. Environment control is essential to maintaining the integrity of the system configuration.

Table 11-4 provides an overview of the four phases of testing. To ensure a thorough test, real-life examples (or scenarios) are identified by a wide number of participants and tested one by one. Any issues should be documented, prioritized, and resolved either with the vendor (or by workflow modification) prior to live system operations.

TRAINING AND SUPPORT

Training should be customized to the workflows that have been identified as the best way to use the system in the practice. This requires developing some customized training materials that blend system "how-to" with policy and procedural direction. Training can also be provided in a variety of ways, including:

- **Train-the-Trainer:** Training typically provided by the vendor to the organization.
- **Classroom Style:** Traditional teaching method in which a group of individuals are trained in a classroom-type setting.
- **One-on-One:** A trainer and an end-user meeting in a (usually) short and focused session to address specific skills, such as documentation templates particular to a subspecialty.
- **Team/Partner Training:** It can be advantageous to train small groups of individuals who work closely together, such as physician/nurse partners as they can remind one another of different scenarios and have a tendency to pay attention to different components of the training.

The duration of training and number of trainers required varies depending on the size of the organization. Even in a small practice, though, at least one individual (or partial FTE) should be appointed as the trainer to ensure consistency

Table 11-4: Testing Phases

Phase	Description and Process
Unit	• Ensures that each aspect of the design has been met (and that the design makes sense) • Accomplished by reviewing all screens and drop-downs • Results in identification of gaps or overlaps
Integrated	• Ensures that the system and policies and procedures can address the majority of conditions in the live environment • Accomplished by creating scenarios for test conditions, documenting mock exams on test patients, and reviewing results • Results in refinement of interfaces, templates, and processes
Stress	• Ensures that the interface can function in a timely manner under maximum load • Accomplished by timing how long it took the system or a component (such as an interface) to respond • Results in determining whether hardware and network are adequate
Parallel	• Compares data in the paper environment to data on the system, to ensure accuracy • May be part of an integrated test (for example, using "real" data as test scenarios) • Results in providing confidence in the system prior to live

PRE-LIVE PREPARATION

Prior to live use of the system, the practice should:

• Ensure that all system testing has been completed and that all major issues have been resolved.

• Transition from the "testing" or "training" system environment to the "live" or "production" system environment. Double-check that all system components are working appropriately (including any uploads, interfaces, and conversions).

• Create user IDs and passwords. Ensure that their system access is appropriate to their roles within the organization, and that only a limited (one to two) number of individuals have access to make changes to the system configuration.

• Have a plan for the go-live day, week, and month. The plan should include a practice or pre-live event, notice to patients and individuals at other locations, and appropriate staffing both on site and at the IS department to support end-users and trouble calls. Consider reducing the schedules for providers for the first week or few weeks of the implementation to provide adequate time to get accustomed to using the new system.

• Begin scanning and/or abstracting key pieces of information from upcoming visits into the EHR so that it is available when the patients arrive at the clinic and reduces overall provider documentation time.

• Make sure to meet with key individuals (including supervisors, lead staff, and all clinicians) at the go-live site to review and discuss the activities of the go-live date so that everyone is well prepared and knows whom to contact with any issues that arise.

GO-LIVE SUPPORT

To support a phased implementation, training is provided for each function just before it is used. At go-live, trainers and IS support staff are available to assist users with any issues that might arise, from resetting passwords to troubleshooting technical issues. Some common tips for a smooth go-live include:

- Choose the go-live date wisely. Mondays are typically very busy days for clinics.
- Bribe users (and patients) with food. Pizza or cookies are a great cure for the headaches caused by using a new system.
- Make sure that the support team is easily identifiable.
- Plan on having at least one support individual for every six system users.

At the conclusion of each day, make sure that the team has an opportunity to debrief, document any issues, and make modifications in preparation for the next day.

POST-LIVE TRAINING AND SUPPORT

The time frame after which each clinic transitions to "normal" post-live support varies. However day-to-day hand-holding generally ends within a few weeks of the live date. After the system has been live for a few weeks (but before system acceptance and delivery of the final milestone payment), perform a post-live survey to identify any issues with system configuration, response time, or user skills. Regular sessions should be scheduled to share tips and identify enhancement needs. On-going support of the system on the smallest scale can consist of a single individual to train users, configure the system, and manage all support. At the most complex level, this can be a group of individuals whose responsibilities range from help desk support, to training, application management, and technical support. While the total time for implementation can range from three months for a small practice to up to a year for a large group's initial go-live, thorough planning and structured implementation will help avoid common mistakes.

Case Study 16: Eight-Year-Old EHR Continues to Evolve

Organization:	Evans Medical Group, Evans, Georgia
Physicians:	3
Active Patients:	12,000
Type:	Multi-specialty Ambulatory Practice

Evans Medical Group is a multi-specialty group in Evans, Georgia, consisting of pediatrics, internal medicine, family practitioners, and clinical and administrative support staff. Nearly everyone in this clinic of 20 FTEs uses the EHR, which was implemented eight years ago. According to Dr. Rob Lamberts, implementation of the EHR has been an evolving process over the eight years that continues even today. Presently, the practice is implementing an interface to a new practice management system and may soon implement an internet hookup to enable them to communicate via secure messaging with patients. Dr. Lamberts also advises that using the EHR required a combination of understanding how the product worked, customizing it to meet the needs of the practice, and then evaluating their workflows and redesigning how the office runs to meet the system. Essentially, there was an ebb and flow. Additionally, the physicians at Evans Medical Group did not care if all data was on the computer; their goal was not computerization, but running the best practice possible.

With an initial investment of approximately $60,000 in 1997, Evans has now moved to a new office which has no space for paper charts. Data from local hospitals is scanned by a full-time telephone operator who also does scanning while on the telephone. EKG and spirometry are interfaced to the EHR, as are the practice management system and community lab. Hospital laboratory data is entered into the system manually, until an interface can be provided by the hospital.

Continued implementation of the system was accomplished by part-time efforts of two physicians and an office manager. Initially, there were challenges in getting all providers to use the system. One doctor would leave the exam room and go to his office to type instead of doing it in the room. After simply increasing the speed of computers in the exam room, the physician started using the system about 90% of the time during the patient exam. Evans Medical Group has been recognized as a HIMSS Davies Award winner due to their excellence in computerization.

Case Study 17: Practice Realizes Quick Physician Adoption

Organization:	Ogden Clinic, Ogden, Utah
Physicians:	54
Type:	Multi-specialty Ambulatory Practice

Founded in 1950, the Ogden Clinic is a multi-specialty clinic in Ogden, Utah. In addition to providing primary care services, Ogden also serves as a referral center for specialty coverage throughout the region. Ogden implemented an EHR in 2004 to advance its ultimate goal of becoming a paperless practice. To overcome the barriers to implementation, clinic administrators focused on four key areas: system phasing and rollout, encounter documentation templates, physician phasing, and training and support.

System Phasing and Rollout

Prior to rollout, clinic staff entered basic patient information—medications, allergies, chronic conditions and medical history—into the EHR rather than scanning complete charts. At their first visit, patients then completed a data sheet, which clerks stationed in the waiting room used to augment the skeleton chart. When the physician entered the exam room, the EHR was already populated with up-to-date, pertinent health information. This approach meant that important patient data appeared in the correct fields from Day One and that the record was uncluttered and accessible. Because physicians could easily find vital information, they immediately saw how effective the EHR system could be.

Encounter Documentation Templates

Clinic staff designated as "super users" entered 40-50 past patient visits into the EHR before implementation to help identify key phrases and charting habits each physician relied upon. Once pinpointed, these phrases and habits were added to the menu of check boxes—making the EHR template familiar and immediately useable for physicians. Providing check boxes that reflected physicians' charting styles sped adoption of the EHR. Within a month, the majority of physicians had gained a half-hour a day to spend seeing more patients.

Physician Phasing

Ogden's physicians were brought on to the EHR system one at a time, with each allowed to progress at his or her own pace. For example, a physician might use the EHR for a handful of patients on the first day and more each day after.

Because the physicians were not overwhelmed by the robust EHR capabilities, they were less resistant to the technology, adjusted to the system quickly, and exhibited greater satisfaction with the transition process.

Training and Support

During initial training sessions, physicians were given access to a straightforward mock patient visit that mimicked the flow and format of the EHR template. After completing a simple encounter, physicians entered the same visit, adding lab orders. They repeated the visit once again, this time adding x-rays and an office service. In addition, after the EHR system was implemented, trainers shadowed the medical assistants and the physician for the first 20 or so visits, helping them adjust to the flow of the EHR software and noting areas to modify templates for ease of use. Overall, these training approaches accomplished two goals: (1) they encouraged physicians to adopt the workflow inherent in the software rather than revert to their dictation-based patterns; and (2) they deterred physicians from requesting onerous adaptations to the template and software structure. This resulted in fewer customizations to the EHR and greater efficiency during the go-live process.

In June 2004, Ogden Clinic brought its first physician onto the EHR. By January 2005, 36 of the clinic's 54 physicians were using the EHR for 100% of their patient visits with no loss of productivity. Ogden administrators have experienced significant decreases in medical record, transcription, supplies and related staffing costs. At the same time, shifts in workflow have allowed staff to identify revenue opportunities—such as noting and scheduling health maintenance visits when patients are seen for other reasons. As a result, Ogden has realized an addition of $50,000 to the bottom line each month (or $600,000 a year) in combined cost savings and revenue enhancements and anticipates this figure will rise to $1 million in 2005.

CHAPTER 12

Making Your EHR Your Legal Health Record

Cheryl Servais, MPH, and Kathy J. Westhafer, RHIA, CHPS

Provider organizations fall into two camps when considering their EHR as their legal health record. Some assume any part of the record that is electronic is also part of the legal record without considering if basic standards for electronic documentation are being met. Others convert major parts of their documentation to electronic format but never take the next step to certify it as part of the LHR, creating parallel processes and costly duplication. This chapter explores the requirements for enabling EHR systems and data to become part of the official LHR.

CHARACTERISTICS OF THE LEGAL HEALTH RECORD

The legal health record (LHR) serves many purposes that do not change simply because a healthcare provider has switched the media for creating and maintaining the medical record from paper to electronic. All information that meets the definition of a medical record or designated record set is part of the legal health record. This information may be generated, captured, and/or stored electronically; however, to become part of the LHR, EHR-generated "documents" must meet the same standards as their hardcopy predecessors. To appreciate this requires an understanding of what the medical record is and the standards that have evolved for it over the last 20 years.

ROLE OF THE MEDICAL RECORD

The role of the medical record is to:
- Communicate information used in making decisions about maintaining a patient's health status or returning the patient to a healthy status;
- Support claims for reimbursement for services provided;

- Improve health care through the provision of case studies and statistical data abstracted directly from the record that can be used for analysis of patient care quality, provider education, and research into new diagnostic and treatment methods; and
- Provide legal documentation of the decisions made and actions taken in response to patient health issues.

DEFINITIONS

The most widely accepted definition of a medical record is contained in the Department of Health and Human Services publication, *Conditions of Participation for Hospitals,*[1] which states "The medical record contains sufficient information to identify the patient, support the diagnosis, justify the treatment, document the course and results, and promote the continuity of care among healthcare providers."

However, the HIPAA Privacy Rule Standards expand this definition with the concept of a "designated record set." The preamble of the rule states that a designated record set includes medical and billing records and any other records used in whole or in part to make decisions about an individual.[2] The "other records" referred to include the records from other providers used to make decisions about an individual (e.g., outside diagnostic tests, physician office records, etc.). The definitions of the record drive the systems, content, and elements to be included in the legal health record.

REGULATIONS AND STANDARDS GOVERNING ELEMENTS FOR A MEDICAL RECORD

In order to meet these purposes, various organizations have prescribed the elements to be included in the medical record.

The federal government sets forth its requirements in the various Conditions of Participation guidances.[1] Additional federal requirements may be found in the Federal Rules of Evidence, Article VIII, which provide guidelines for records to be admissible in a federal court. In addition, most states have requirements for medical record content, usually as part of hospital or other provider licensing laws. Although generally in agreement with the federal provisions, differences can exist.

Finally, accrediting bodies such as the Joint Commission on Accreditation of Health Care Organizations (JCAHO),[3] American Osteopathic Association, Accreditation Association for Ambulatory Healthcare, and Commission on Accreditation of Rehabilitation Facilities have standards that address the content of a medical record. The HL7 EHR standards relevant to the LHR are presented in Table 12-1.

FACILITY CONSIDERATIONS IN DEFINING THE LEGAL HEALTH RECORD

The expanded definition of a health record published in the HIPAA Standards for Privacy requires facilities to develop a description of their legal health record. Beyond the clinical requirements stated in federal or state regulations or in the standards

Table 12-1: The HL7 EHR Prescription*

Health record information and management (I.2)	Manage EHR information across EHR-S applications by ensuring that clinical information entered by providers is a valid representation of clinical notes; and is accurate and complete according to clinical rules and tracking amendments to clinical document.
Data retention, availability and destruction (I.2.1)	Retain, ensure availability, and destroy health record information according to organizational standards.
Audit trail (I.2.2)	Provide audit trail capabilities for resource access and usage indicating the author, the modification (where pertinent), and the date and time at which a record was created, modified, viewed, extracted, or deleted.
Synchronization (I.2.3)	Maintain synchronization involving: interaction with entity directories; linkage of received data with existing entity records; location of each health record component; and communication of changes between key systems.

*For a comprehensive and current list of HL7 EHR standard components visit www.hl7.org/ehr.

of various agencies, a facility must determine what other records are used to make decisions about individuals. Potential documents to include are:

1. Minimum Data Set databases in long term care facilities;
2. Patient maintained records;
3. E-mails between patient and provider;
4. Radiographic films or images;
5. Wave forms (e.g., EKG or EEG or fetal monitor tracings);
6. Photographs, videotapes;
7. Patient records or data from other providers;
8. Online alerts and responses;
9. Secondary databases (e.g., abstract data, quality data, registry data).

The American Health Information Management Association (AHIMA) has recently issued a Practice Brief that provides guidelines for facilities in defining the elements of their legal health record.[4]

CREATING A "HYBRID" LEGAL HEALTH RECORD

A facility may elect to maintain separate files for electronic and nonelectronic components of the LHR. This option is often referred to as a "hybrid" medical record as it is a combination of different storage media (online systems, paper, film, etc.).

The definition of a hybrid medical record is similar to that of the legal medical record. AHIMA defines the hybrid record as one that "comprises individually identifiable data, in any medium, that are collected, processed, stored, displayed, and used by healthcare professionals. The information in the health record is collected and/or directly used to document healthcare delivery or healthcare status."[5]

Developing a "hybrid" LHR involves three steps: revising corporate policy and process, inventorying sources of the components of the LHR, and qualifying EHR components as part of the LHR.

UPDATING CORPORATE HEALTH INFORMATION MANAGEMENT POLICY AND PROCESS

Health Information Management (HIM) departments have historically been responsible for the policies that outline the maintenance, use, disclosure, and retention of the medical record. As the EHR evolves, policies surrounding these same issues must be reviewed and updated. New policies are also likely to be needed. In particular, a policy outlining the hybrid LHR, its development and content, is important. An LHR policy will provide clear direction and guidance to those developing and using and disclosing the record.

Efforts to revise corporate policy should engage the key stakeholders from the organization. Include representatives from clinical areas (nursing and physicians in particular), IT, HIM, and legal. Expect to spend some time educating the group on background, purpose, and objectives, as a LHR policy will be new ground. Before drafting changes, be sure to research any federal, state, or accreditation requirements as well as HL7 standards that will determine criteria the information or system will need to meet. These criteria will include language regarding tracking of history of revisions to documents and information, standards for documentation, and authentication and fidelity of interfaced systems. Most important is that the policy and related procedure be clear and understandable to everyone in the organization.

Other items to outline within the policy, or as a separate procedure, include the process by which individual pieces of the record will be approved as part of the LHR. If, for example, the intensive care unit has a documentation system, how will the electronic information it captures become designated as part of the LHR? Is there an additional committee needed to evaluate each system and make the determination of the LHR? Can the responsibilities of an already existing committee be expanded, such as a forms committee? Finally, statements in the policy that address printing will help to provide further guidance.

As with any policy, communication is key. Be sure to provide education to pertinent areas and designate a few experts within the organization who can work directly with sponsors of the information to walk them through the process and explain concepts. Review the policy on a regular basis. The EHR/LHR standards are still very much in development and will continue to evolve over the next few years.

DEVELOPING AN INVENTORY OF THE LHR

Providers using a hybrid LHR should develop an inventory of the various components of the LHR and their status as part of the EHR. It should also include the "source system" and the "EHR system." The source system is where the information is originally created in electronic format. The EHR system is the system the clinician uses to access the information. In some cases these are the same such as when a nursing assessment is entered online into the EHR. In other instances they are different, such as with lab data that originates in the lab system but is interfaced over to the EHR system used by the clinician. A limited example of such an inventory is provided in Table 12-2. Sometimes the storage media can be difficult to determine if there are both paper and electronic versions of the information. This might occur with laboratory results that are maintained electronically and printed and placed in the file. Such an occurrence raises a red flag about which medium is to be regarded the "source of truth" (see "Process Issues with the Hybrid Record" below).

Table 12-2: LHR/EHR Inventory

Document	EHR Status	Source System / EHR System	Date EHR Started
History and physical exam report	EHR	Transcription system / EHR system	1/1/2002
Nursing assessment	EHR	EHR system	3/15/2004
Laboratory text result	EHR	Laboratory information system via results reporting system	6/15/1998
Advanced directive	Paper filed in chart	NA	NA

QUALIFYING EHR INFORMATION AS THE LHR

Many organizations believe that once a paper document can be replaced with an electronic one, that the new electronic document is the LHR. Before the electronic version can be certified as part of the EHR, and included in the LHR inventory as such, it should be scrutinized to ensure that it meets the basic criteria provided in Table 12-3.

Furthermore, not all components of the EHR are part of the LHR. Some EHR elements such as work lists are essentially a communication mechanism and are not part of the LHR. Other systems may not be part of the LHR because they collect or filter data "up-stream" of the primary source of information used by clinicians, such as glucometers that collect and store clinical information that is ultimately fed to the laboratory system.

Table 12-3: Checklist for LHR Qualifying Electronic Documents*

EHR originated documents must:
- ☑ Be the primary source used by clinicians
- ☑ Allow for electronic signatures and include a nonrepudiation feature
- ☑ Allow for the ability to print online documents for correspondence, legal matters (e.g. subpoenas), outside reviewers, etc.
- ☑ Strictly control the "uncharting" or deletion of documents/data
- ☑ Have capability/capacity to store records for the legal time required
- ☑ Utilize acceptable clinical terminology

EHR interfaced documents must be:
- ☑ Linked to the correct patient/encounter
- ☑ Reported (not truncated) with as little manipulation as possible
- ☑ Reconciled to ensure that all transmissions are completed without loss of data, documents or records

* EHR components qualifying as part of the LHR must meet the criteria in this table at a minimum.

SCANNING

Today, many organizations scan hardcopy documents from the LHR after discharge. This is done primarily to enhance access, storage, and reproduction of paper-based documents. These systems can provide a valuable bridge while other EHR systems are being developed. Given that these systems meet the LHR definitions, they would be considered in the hybrid LHR solution.

PROCESS ISSUES WITH THE HYBRID RECORD

As the saying goes, *the devil is in the details*. Providers face a myriad of process issues related to the migration from paper to electronic records. For example, there are times, such as in the case of a patient-initiated pain assessment, in which a document may first be created on paper, followed by data entry into the EHR. In this case, the issue to be resolved is: which document is the LHR and should the two documents be synchronized? In the example of the pain assessment, the form might be completed by the patient prior to the visit and then reviewed by the provider during the visit. Once the provider has validated the information, it is entered into the EHR and authenticated electronically by the provider. In this instance, the LHR will be the EHR. There is no need to retain the paper document completed by the patient and therefore no need to keep the documents in conformity. Any updates to the information will be made in the system.

In contrast, a different outcome occurs if the provider makes his or her notations on the paper document completed by the patient, signs it, and then forwards it to a clerical person to perform the data entry function within the EHR. In this situation, the paper document would be the legal document, since it is what has been reviewed and authenticated. Strong consideration should be given to keeping the two documents synchronized, so that regardless of the source of the data accessed (paper or electronic), the information would be the same.

These examples are fairly straightforward, but clearly demonstrate that with similar circumstances, significantly different decisions may be made. The key point in making any LHR determination is to understand the processes surrounding the documentation.

PRINTING

Another process issue to consider is the extent to which electronic documents will be printed. There are some users who find glancing through a paper medical record more convenient than navigating through an electronic one. The attending physician may want to have the consultant's report with him or her when speaking with the patient. In this paper-to-electronic transition period, paper charts are not at all uncommon.

The problem with printing information and placing it in the chart is that not only does this process perpetuate dependence on the paper chart, but having multiple sources for the information makes defining the "source of truth" unclear. The paper document may be written on and updated without making it consistent with the electronic record. Likewise, the electronic documentation may have been updated without reprinting the information. In either case the provider risks acting on old or outdated information. If for some reason printing is required, clear procedures must be in place to ensure that the document is not updated and is destroyed in a secure manner after use (e.g. shredded).

CLOSING THE RECORD

Closing or completing the record may also provide some process challenges. In the paper-based world, the in-patient record was removed from the floor, brought to the health information management (HIM) department, and processed. Physicians would be notified of medical record deficiencies and would then visit the department and be presented with the specific chart to complete. Chances of documentation occurring on the "wrong" patient encounter were minimal as access to the record was limited. The EHR allows for improved access to information and electronic record completion can benefit the physician in many ways. The risk lies with the benefit. Because of improved access, the risk of documenting on the wrong encounter or even the wrong patient is higher. Facilities should review and determine what processes can and should be put in place to mitigate the risk. Should updates to records be controlled after discharge? Should there be a notification process in place if updates or additions to the record occur after a specified time period from discharge that someone would review? There is no one "right" answer; processes must be evaluated in order to make the best decision for the facility.

INFORMATION REQUESTS

The final process issue to be discussed here is that of responding to requests for information. Even if the facility's records are electronic, a purely electronic release process, whereby the record can be electronically packaged and transmitted, will not work in all situations. Requestors cannot universally receive and process information sent in this manner. In addition, there are security issues to resolve which may be resource intensive on both the requestor's and facility's part.

Although some organizations may choose to print all electronic documents after discharge and create a paper chart or add to one that already exists, the risk of this alternative is a question as to the source of the legal record and timeliness of the information provided. The recommended alternative, however, is to maintain the EHR as the legal record and print it when requested. The benefit of this process is that not only does it maintain the integrity of the LHR, but it will likely also minimize the dependence on and use of paper.

Case Study 18: Designing with the Legal Health Record in Mind

Organization:	Christiana Care Health System, Wilmington, Delaware
Acute Care Facilities:	2
Staffed Beds:	1,000
Type:	Community Hospital with Residency Program

Christiana Care's Helen F. Graham Cancer Center has provided over 60,000 patient visits since the doors opened in 2002. The Multidisciplinary Disease Centers located there give patients the opportunity to see a surgeon, medical oncologist, and radiation oncologist all in one visit, with other resources and services provided when appropriate. This facility was built with the idea that medical records would be maintained electronically, streamlining documentation, facilitating communication and sharing of information.

Initially, records created by the multidisciplinary centers were paper-based and scanned into Christiana Care's document imaging system. While this met the objective of eliminating long term storage and retrieval of a paper medical record and provided ample access to the records, it did little to streamline the documentation process or minimize the record management functions.

In order to meet all the objectives, work began on development of online forms that could be completed and signed by the provider. A process had been set up to review electronic forms through the Functional Documentation Committee that can be likened to an "electronic forms committee." Members of this group include not only IT staff but individuals representing HIM, legal, and clinical along with the form sponsor attending. Forms are usually presented at several stages of their development:

- Conceptual Review: Review needs and potential for duplication of information collected.
- Build Review: Review initial design and implementation and auditing process outlined.
- Final Review: Last look and "tweaking" before implementation.

One of the first Cancer Center forms considered was the Cancer Center Medical History. This particular form is sent to the patient for return to the Center prior to his or her visit. Data entry is then performed. At the time of the visit, the nurse reviews the information with the patient. Once the information is verified, the nurse electronically signs the form. No paper record is maintained. Any further modifications are made via the electronic form that provides appropriate auditing capability. Based on processes outlined and the auditing provided through the system, the Committee felt comfortable in designating this and other similar forms as a portion of the LHR.

Learning how to analyze electronic documentation systems presented the most significant challenge to implementation. Facilities just beginning on this road should not expect easy answers, but by pursuing answers to the multitude of questions, the organization will have not only an electronic medical record but one which is also legally sound.

References

1   Department of Health and Human Services. 42 CFR Part 2 §482.24(c), Conditions of Participation for Hospitals. Available at http://www.access.gpo.gov/nara/cfr/waisidx_99/42cft482_99.html.

2   Standards for Privacy of Individually Identifiable Health Information, Final Rule. 45 CFR Parts 160 and 164. 65 Federal Register 250 (December 28, 2000). Available at http://aspe.hhs.gov/adminsimp.

3   Joint Commission on Accreditation of Healthcare Organizations. *2004 Hospital Accreditation Standards.* Oakbrook Terrace, IL: Joint Commissions on Accreditation of Healthcare Organizations, 2004.

4   American Health Information Management Association. *Practice Brief: Definition of the Health Record for Legal Purposes.* Chicago: AHIMA. Available at www.ahima.org

5   American Health Information Management Association. *Practice Brief: Complete Medical Record in a Hybrid EHR Environment: Part I: Managing the Transition.* Chicago: AHIMA; 2003. Available at www. AHIMA.org.

CHAPTER 13

EHR Technical Architecture

Martin L. Zola

For most organizations, the journey toward the EHR involves the implementation of an array of software products needed to deliver the complex functionality described in the previous chapters. The potential mixing and matching of vendor- and locally-developed software could produce an almost infinite number of configurations. This chapter describes how to plan an EHR architecture and how to address architecturally the EHR's unique features.

As pointed out in the previous chapters, EHRs are introducing dramatic changes to the healthcare environment. Paper records are being phased out as electronic information capture and sharing become more widespread. Caregivers, who previously viewed the EHR as an adjunct resource, are now realizing it is an essential and commonplace component of the process of delivering care. Organizations, once the "owner" of clinical and administrative data, are now becoming stewards of a larger data infrastructure that spans corporate and geographical boundaries.

The traditional clinical systems architecture is being stretched to accommodate a new set of demands:

- Wireless requirements are expanding as point-of-care clinical documentation grows.
- The distinction between the EHR and medical devices is blurring as the measurements of the devices are regarded as just another type of clinical data.
- The availability of online clinical data outside the facility in physician offices and even for patient access is often assumed.
- Demands for sharing information and interoperability are growing.

Stephen R. Smith contributed Case Study 19 on IT and Medical Device Convergence. Ted Bailey contributed Case Study 20 on Infrastructure Endures Hurricane.

- The almost ubiquitous use of the EHR demands a new level of availability and recoverability.

With these changes in mind, this chapter introduces techniques for good architecture planning and design. The paragraphs that follow explain the fundamental concepts and then describe how to apply the concepts to practical situations. While the responsibility for developing the technical architecture usually rests with the IT organization or consultants, the goal here is to give non-IT decision makers an understanding of the concepts so that they can ask the right questions and determine if the right decisions are being made.

PLAN THE ARCHITECTURE: DO NOT LEAVE THINGS TO CHANCE

Like an iceberg, much of an EHR lies hidden beneath the surface in its architecture. To achieve success, the architecture should be planned and not allowed to unfold without direction. This means that the team needs to assess the architecture that is currently in place and determine the types of changes that are necessary to support both tactical and strategic EHR projects. The end result of this analysis should be a document describing the new or updated architecture. This document is referred to as an architecture specification.

To make it easier to deal with the complexities of the architecture, the specification is usually arrayed in "layers" of related information. The layers are generally arranged from the conceptual to the operational. Six layers, in particular, stand out in describing most EHRs. They are: functional descriptions, data descriptions, hardware/software components, security infrastructure, operational support, and provisions for business continuity/disaster recovery.

These layers vary in content depending upon the specific situation. The checklist shown in Table 13-1 lists the type of information that should be considered for inclusion in the layers of the architecture.

The organization should begin drafting the architecture specification as early as possible and continue to update the specification as new EHR requirements and components are considered. Not all of the information indicated in Table 13-1 is required in every case. Typically, the specifications can be captured in less than 50 pages, and the team can compact the information into tables and other space-saving structures.

Once the architecture specification has been defined, it can serve as a guide to the teams that are implementing the EHR. The architecture specification also allows the organization to assess, before component systems are acquired or implemented, whether there is a good fit between the planned solution and the architecture. If prepared properly, the specification should exhibit an appropriate balance of function, performance, and cost.

Table 13-1: EHR Technical Architecture Specification Checklist

Layer	Contents	
Functional	• Statement of scope	• Functional requirements
Data	• Data descriptions • Data archiving strategy	• Data exchanges with external systems
Technical components	• Commercial hardware & software • In-house custom-developed software • Clinical devices interfaces	• Storage systems • Network components
Security	• Preventative measures • Detection measures	• Assurance measures • Forensics measures
Support	• Provisioning • Training	• Bug fixes & version updates • System administration
Continuity & recovery	• Backup & recovery procedures • Secured off-site data storage	• Down-time contingency procedures • Recovery & continuity procedures

ARCHITECTURE OPTIONS FOR CARE-PROVIDING ORGANIZATIONS

Most EHR architectures fall within a few common architectural classes: centralized architectures, N-tier architectures, and Web-based architectures. Figure 13-1 provides a graphical summary of the types of architecture options.

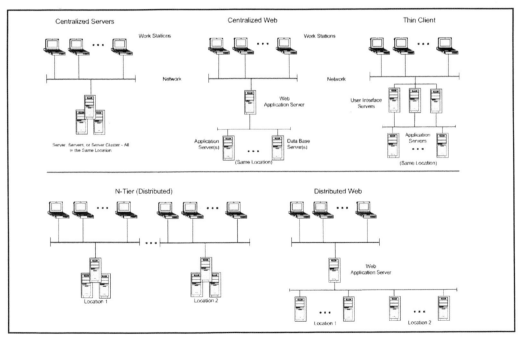

Figure 13-1: EHR Architecture Options

CENTRALIZED ARCHITECTURES

A centralized architecture is characterized by having all of the processing and data storage being performed at one location. Users are connected to the central resources via the network. All processing is done on the central server(s), and the central server(s) manage(s) the application databases.

A second type of centralized architecture is based upon thin client technology (as implemented by products such as Citrix MetaFrame and Microsoft Terminal Server). Thin client is becoming increasingly popular with healthcare organizations supporting large numbers of user workstations that are physically dispersed across a wide geographic area. With thin client architectures, central servers provide and control the user interface at the desktop. To the users, it looks as if the application is running on their PCs, but in fact the processing and interfaces are emanating from the servers.

N-Tier Architectures

In an N-Tier architecture, workstations access application servers to obtain EHR and clinical information. There may be a separate server for each application. The application servers receive and process requests from workstations and during the processing of those requests a server may send requests to another application server or to a database server. In this configuration users often must have special client software installed on their workstations in order to access the desired application servers. This client software enables the workstation to do some processing locally on the workstation which has the benefit of improving response time and performance. (When client software is used in this fashion, this is often called a client server configuration.)

If the application servers are located together in the same place, this is referred to as being a centralized N-Tier configuration. If the application and database servers are situated at physically different locations (and sometimes outside the enterprise), this is referred to as a distributed N-Tier architecture.

Web-based Architectures

A Web-based architecture is characterized by one or more Web servers that act as the front-end for users who are seeking application services. Users connect to the Web server by launching their browsers and entering the URL (if it is not automatically preset) of the entry page. From there on, the user and the Web server interact via Web pages.

Behind the scenes, the Web server and the application servers may be one platform or separate platforms, and these servers may be physically co-located (i.e., centralized) or dispersed to different locations (distributed). In a Web -based approach, the processing can be done 100% by the servers (i.e., thin client), or the Web server may download an applet or script to the workstation browser where it executes (distributed processing). The Web architecture greatly reduces the labor required to maintain and administer desktops. This can be a major savings in large organizations with thousands of desktops (or for organizations with desktops that are located at a distance from the desktop support team).

The trend today in large healthcare environments is toward Web-based, N-Tier, and thin client architectures. These architectures provide the flexibility to accommodate most applications needed and can be scaled cost-effectively to meet the organization's processing needs. However, the variations among these architectures still present a formidable challenge to organizations that are attempting to determine the architecture type that best meets their needs. The next two sections provide specific guidance in crafting architectures for private practices, clinics, and larger organizations.

ARCHITECTURES FOR THE AMBULATORY SETTING

Most private practices and ambulatory clinics share several common characteristics that render the IT infrastructure for an EHR fairly straightforward:

- The practice is generally located in one building or in nearby facilities.
- The practice is usually focused on some common forms of care such as family medicine, specialized medicine, outpatient surgery, and the like.
- The number of users and user workstations is generally small, often fewer than 25 and rarely more than 100.

Because of the number, locations, and types of devices and the circumscribed nature of the treatment being provided, the resulting architecture is relatively simple and straightforward. Thus, a relatively small number of commercial hardware and software packages can be assembled to meet the needs of the entire organization. Given these common characteristics, it is clear that the centralized server and the centralized Web-based architectures are well suited for private practice and small ambulatory organizations.

A hypothetical configuration for a private practice might consist of one or more servers in a protected area connected via an in-house network to PCs and laptops in the practice areas. Workstations are placed in treatment areas, provider offices, and business areas. Special displays may be required (e.g., for diagnostic imaging). The network would most likely be wired; however, a secured wireless network may be feasible for low-volume data exchanges. Application software, such as practice management, EHR, billing, office automation, and e-mail, is hosted on the centralized servers and some PCs. Chances are this software comes from the same or compatible vendors so the software interoperates well. The practice should also have a reliable Internet service provider. Providers can use a Virtual Private Network (VPN) from home or other locations. If the practice establishes an interface to the Internet or allows dial-up connections, a firewall will be necessary to protect the network at these interfaces.

Some private practices may not be comfortable hosting this type of internal IT infrastructure. Fortunately, there are an abundance of vendors that will (for a fee) administer and operate the EHR or provide access via the Internet to an EHR application running at their data center (the latter is referred to as an application service provider or ASP). The case for outsourcing the EHR infrastructure (or going with an ASP) lies in trading off asset ownership for peace of mind at a price. The case for hosting internally boils down to greater control over IT resources, flexibility, and potential costs savings.

Finally, disaster recovery is an important ingredient in designing the private practice architecture. Fortunately, in most cases the recovery solution is very manageable. The practice should choose hardware components that are readily available in the market-place. In the event of a disaster, replacement components can be shipped to the practice within hours. Second, the practice must ensure that all software and data are backed up in accordance with a rock-solid backup procedure and stored in safe containers at an appropriate offsite location. The backup media should be stored several miles away at a location that is outside the risk zone of the operational site. Third, the recovery procedures must be documented and the practice should have a contract established with an IT resource to respond immediately to perform the recovery, if necessary.

ARCHITECTURES FOR LARGER INSTITUTIONS

Virtually all large healthcare organizations have entrenched IT infrastructures. It is also likely that within these legacy infrastructures some of the elements of an EHR may already be in place such as laboratory, pharmacy and order communication systems.

The challenge for the larger institutions is to determine how to integrate the existing, although possibly diverse, EHR elements and introduce new components to achieve the overall desired functionality. This means determining what new functions to implement, what mechanisms (existing and new) to use to support the EHR functions, and how to orchestrate the elements to interoperate and share data effectively. Some organizations may be able to extend the capabilities of existing products to achieve the desired range of EHR functionality. However, many, if not most large organizations will need to develop effective ways of adding new capabilities and integrating these new capabilities across their heterogeneous configuration of products. Such products need to interact so that they appear to be one logical, coordinated application.

Organizations will need a modular and flexible architecture to accommodate these new capabilities. The best architecture types to achieve this flexibility are:
- N-Tier centralized or distributed
- Web-based centralized or distributed
- Thin client

An N-Tier architecture will allow the organization to add new workstations and servers and build the logic that connects the components into a seamless service. N-Tier allows the organization to add just the right amount of computing power when and where it is needed. If the organization is large and spread out over several geographically dispersed facilities, the N-Tier architecture will allow the organization to locate servers closer to users. This has the advantage of reducing communications costs and improving response times. It also has a secondary benefit of enabling the organization to host its own disaster recovery site if the distributed servers can serve as fall back servers in the event of a disaster at another server location.

A Web-based architecture is similar to N-Tier in that servers can be added as new functionality is needed. One major difference is that with Web-based architectures, users interact with their applications exclusively through their browsers. No software is installed on user PCs and workstations. Web servers manage the user interface for the user and pass processing requests to application servers that may be located anywhere. Web architectures make it easier to integrate legacy applications with new applications and each other because the Web server can provide a single interface that ties all of the legacy applications together into one logical unit.

Finally, disaster recovery for complicated data centers can be a major undertaking and very expensive. Most healthcare organizations have not adequately addressed disaster recovery planning. However, HIPAA and JCAHO have forced disaster recovery to the forefront. The traditional approach in other industries is to contract for an offsite backup data center or to arrange for a mobile response such as a tractor trailer configured with servers, workstations, networks, cabling, and portable power generation prepared to drive to the site in the event of a disaster. These arrangements can be very expensive and not likely to include all applications. Consequently, many healthcare organizations are considering implementing their own backup data centers. This is discussed in greater detail in the next section.

OTHER ARCHITECTURAL CONSIDERATIONS

The above sections covered the fundamentals of architecture planning. The following sections examine some of the options for keeping infrastructure costs low and for implementing features that are special to the EHR.

Techniques for Controlling Architecture Costs

Here are several techniques for holding down the architecture costs:

- *Reduce the heterogeneity in the architecture:* Wherever practical, minimize the variations in the type of hardware platforms, operating systems, application vendors, and databases. This will simplify the complexity of the architecture and lower the level of technical skills required to administer it. Generally, this reduces administrative labor requirements and the cost per staff member (salary).

- *Centralize the architecture as much as possible:* Centralizing also reduces the complexity in the architecture and reduces the labor involved in maintaining it. This is because the staff has less geographical area to cover, and there is less time lost due to traveling to equipment sites. In some geographically dispersed organizations, the communications costs and response time latencies may necessitate some equipment distribution.

- *Use readily available commercial components:* Commercial products that are sold as commodities are generally better values, and professionals who work with these components are easier to find (and less expensive to hire). In addition, if a disaster forces an organization to make a large quantity purchase, replacements are usually available within hours or a few days.

- *Invest in labor-saving mechanisms:* One of the most expensive parts of owning and operating an EHR architecture is the labor it takes to keep it running smoothly. Whenever a tool or technology is available that can lower the need for labor, consider investing in it. This includes tools that allow administrators to remotely monitor the health and status of remote components, perform administrative actions on servers/desktops from a central location, and directory services that enforce consistent operations throughout the enterprise.

Options for Dealing with Infrastructure Disaster

Table 13-2 summarizes the major recovery options applicable to care-providing organizations.

- *Null option (no special recovery provisions):* Instead, plan a speedy recovery. Recovery usually involves salvaging, cleaning up, ordering, and shipping replacement components to the disaster site, and re-installation. The Null Option can work for small, centralized configurations where the surrounding infrastructure is intact and the damaged components are readily available commercially. Also, for this option to work, the organization must have backed-up software and data in accordance with acceptable practice and have previously documented recovery procedures.

• *Contract an external recovery site:* Arrange for a commercial service to provide a temporary recovery site or to send a recovery center on a tractor trailer. This option requires that communications links be established between the healthcare organization and the recovery center. It requires substantial time and testing to transfer the needed applications to the temporary recovery center. The costs can be high and not all applications may be accommodated.

• *Self-hosted cold recovery site:* Set aside an area at a safe location to serve as a standby recovery site. This site must be pre-wired for power and network connectivity and pre-installed with racks, telephone lines, HVAC, and backup power. The site may also be set up with a few servers with the rest to be rush-delivered in the event of a disaster. When a disaster occurs, the servers need to be installed, configured, and connected to the network. The process can take several days.

• *Self-hosted warm or hot recovery site:* A warm site has all the servers needed and network connectivity, but the applications software and data are not installed. Recovery involves installing the applications, restoring the data, and connecting to the network. This usually takes several hours. The hot standby has all the servers needed with the applications and data in place and current to the point of the disaster. In this configuration it takes only a few minutes to switch the applications to online status.

Table 13-2: EHR Disaster Recovery Options

	Null Option	External Recovery Site	Self-Hosted Cold Recovery Site	Self-Hosted Warm Recovery Site	Self-Hosted Hot Recovery Site
Set-up costs	$0 Setup costs	Moderate to high set-up costs	Low set-up costs	Moderate set-up costs	Moderate-to-high set-up costs
Annual operational costs	$0 Annual costs	Moderate to high annual costs	Low annual costs	Moderate annual costs	Moderate-to-high annual costs
Likely Recovery Time	Weeks or months	Hours	Days	Hours	Seconds or minutes
Impact on patient care	Major adverse impact on patient care	Very little impact on patient care	Possibly some impact on patient care	Very little impact on patient care	Unlikely to impact patient care

Most small practices or clinics would find the Null Option or the Self-Hosted Cold Recovery Site Option as the most cost-effective alternatives for their treatment settings. With larger organizations, the decision is usually more complicated. Organizations that are in high risk areas such as hurricane or earthquake prone regions might find that warm and hot self-hosted recovery sites might best meet their needs. Other large organizations with low risk profiles may find that a Self-Hosted Cold Recovery Site may be acceptable. Organizations with multiple data centers may be able to increase resources at one or two key data centers to allow for graceful fail over in the event of the demise of one of the centers.

CONVERGENCE

Historically, information technology departments in the healthcare industry have focused on software applications such as billing, scheduling, and department communication (order entry/results reporting) as well as desktop computers and networks. Biomedical engineering departments have focused on maintaining clinical equipment such as patient care monitors, infusion pumps, and other equipment requiring calibration and ongoing maintenance. As microchip technology has become pervasive, biomedical equipment vendors have begun adding more computational and storage capabilities to their devices.

The recently evolution of healthcare software applications has begun including clinical patient information whether documented by a clinician or generated digitally from medical equipment. The digital clinical information from equipment vendors is often provided in an application developed by the equipment vendor in either a proprietary format which must be manually extracted and added into the traditional IT software solution. Though this has been a great advancement for the clinician and opened up new clinical approaches such as remote radiology PACs reading or remote intensive care patient monitoring, it is still a challenge for an IT department to provide an integrated, single source view for active clinicians.

To bridge this gap, IT department leadership should be involved in early decision making around the selection of bio-medical equipment. The IT representative should be ensuring the equipment vendor can effectively communicate with other systems in use at the hospital. With the growth of malicious software, the vendor must also be providing a technical environment that is able to be protected as well as appropriately backed up. Implementation considerations for IT and medical device convergence are provided in Table 13-3.

Table 13-3: Implementation Considerations around Convergence

☑ Ensure IT is involved in process of selecting medical devices.
☑ Maintain an inventor of all operating-system based equipment
☑ Implement robust procedures around virus protection and patches.
☑ Ensure adequate security for devices maintaining patient information.
☑ Limit access through firewall, no modems allowed.
☑ Have a contingency plan for virus attacks.
☑ Educate bio-engineering department about issues with commercial software.
☑ Educate IT staff about biomedical equipment.

Ultimately, these technologies must converge resulting in a fully integrated system that should improve patient care and clinician access to information. The medication management process is a rich example of a complicated process involving at least three different handoffs (physician, pharmacist, nurse) each interacting with different systems that have historically not communicated well together. Complete convergence and integration is achieved when the physician enters an infusion order into a system that a pharmacist verifies that automatically programs an infusion pump for a nurse to electronically confirm is being administered to the right patient. Today, many of these steps have the added risk of a human programming error.

Case Study 19: IT and Medical Device Convergence

Organization:	Hospital of the University of Pennsylvania, Philadelpha
Acute Care Facilities:	3-hospital, 1,500-bed system
Staffed Beds:	672
Type:	Academic Medical Center

The Hospital of the University of Pennsylvania (HUP) is the 672-bed flagship hospital and medical center of the University of Pennsylvania Health System in Philadelphia, Pennsylvania. Owned completely by the University of Pennsylvania, HUP is the system's major teaching hospital and staffed by physicians with appointments at the University of Pennsylvania School of Medicine. As part of HUP's emphasis on patient safety, the Nursing and Quality department leadership began investigating technology improvements in the high-risk area of infusion pumps. In mid 2003, HUP began a pilot with smart infusion pump technology in a limited ICU setting. These pumps had algorithms and safeguards built into them to notify the nurse if an infusion was programmed at a rate too high or too low for the patient. It also provided alerts for any free flow or bolus-type programming. These alerts could be set to warn the nurse to change the setting or force a change. These pumps were also able to provide the historical information on how the drugs were administered and when staff were warned of inappropriate settings for review and research analysis.

The pumps were quickly accepted by nursing as a significant patient safety improvement and were then implemented throughout the hospital. The time to implementation was several months with most of the clinical effort involved in the agreement around the formulary and the boundaries of the flow settings programmed into the pumps.

After the initial rollout, HUP became an early adopter of wireless technology for these pumps and integrated them into the IT infrastructure. This enabled usage and alert information to be retrieved remotely from the approximately 1,000 pumps and allowed for an automated downloading of updated formulary tables whenever changes were deemed appropriate. This involved close coordination with the IT department to ensure appropriate coverage and security. Overall, the data retrieved from the pumps have demonstrated a reduction in errors in infusion administration. The data have also demonstrated a likelihood for more errors to occur at certain times during the day as well as certain days of the week which has resulted in changes to nursing staffing patterns.

Case Study 20: Infrastructure Endures Hurricanes

Organization:	Bon Secours, Southwest Florida Division
Acute Care Facilities:	2
Staffed Beds:	485
Type:	Community Hospitals

Like many hospitals their size, Bon Secours Venice and Saint Joseph's Hospitals have implemented precursors to an EHR in the form of a paperless patient care system in the ED. Both hospitals are also located in southwest Florida, the region with the highest hurricane risk in the U.S. Recognizing the weather hazards in the region, IT built failover data centers at the hospitals and redundant communication circuits between them. In addition to two separate circuits between data centers (same central telephone office), each data center established separate connections via different central telephone offices to the Internet. Thus, the Internet could serve as a third circuit between the hospitals.

In 2004 the area was devastated by Hurricane Charlie. Venice and Saint Joseph's were the only hospitals in the region that maintained data and voice communications and able to maintain ED services. The data centers continued to provide uninterrupted application services (a significant portion of their application architecture is thin client). As circuits and Internet connections went down, IT was able to switch to alternate circuits. During this time the case load in the ED quadrupled. The ED wouldn't have been able to sustain this volume of services without full and uninterrupted access to its paperless patient care systems. When the National Guard experienced communications problems, the Guard connected to the hospital circuits for more reliable voice and data communications.

In retrospect, IT's planning for the worst case scenario and Bon Secour's willingness to make the additional investment made this a successful outcome. The investment in continuity and resiliency was appreciated by the community when it needed it the most. From a technical perspective, Hurricane Charlie demonstrated that a single communication circuit to a back-up data center is insufficient and that communications links are more vulnerable than data centers. Further, data centers should not be placed near roofs or windows, and organizations should plan to shield IT equipment as water will trickle down from upper floors.

Index